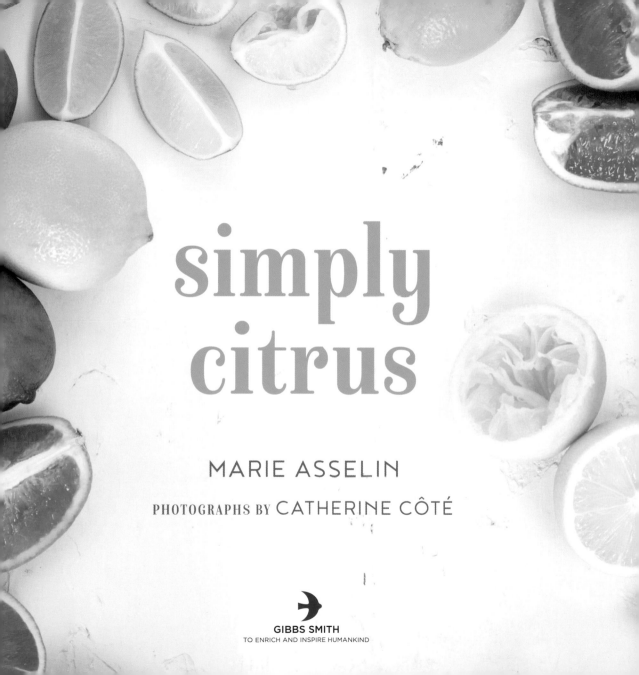

simply citrus

MARIE ASSELIN

PHOTOGRAPHS BY CATHERINE CÔTÉ

GIBBS SMITH
TO ENRICH AND INSPIRE HUMANKIND

To my maman, Réjeane,
who raised me on delicious home-cooked meals.
Thank you for letting me snip fresh herbs,
crack eggs, and lick batters.
You not only gave me life and unconditional love,
but you also gave roots to my future career.
Je t'aime!

First Edition
22 21 20 19 18   5 4 3 2 1

Text © 2018 Marie Asselin
Photographs © 2018 Catherine Côté

Published by
Gibbs Smith
P.O. Box 667
Layton, Utah 84041

1.800.835.4993 orders
www.gibbs-smith.com

Designed by Katie Jennings Campbell
Printed and bound in Hong Kong

Gibbs Smith books are printed on paper produced from sustainable PEFC-certified forest/controlled wood source. Learn more at www.
pefc.org.
Printed and bound in Hong Kong

Library of Congress Cataloging-in-Publication Data

Names: Asselin, Marie, author.
Title: Simply citrus / Marie Asselin ; photographs by Catherine Côté.
Description: First edition. | Layton, Utah : Gibbs Smith, 2017. | Includes
index.
Identifiers: LCCN 2017032574 | ISBN 9781423648130 (Hardcover)
Subjects: LCSH: Cooking (Citrus fruits) | LCGFT: Cookbooks.
Classification: LCC TX813.C5 A87 2017 | DDC 641.6/4304--dc23
LC record available at https://lccn.loc.gov/2017032574

contents

acknowledgments

I WILL FOREVER BE GRATEFUL to my editor, Kerry McShane, who spotted me on Instagram and offered me the chance to publish my first book. I'm sure I'll always look back on the day we met in Québec City as a pivotal moment in my career. Thank you for cheering for me along the way.

Thank you to Michelle Branson, editor and head of the cookbook team at Gibbs Smith. Meeting you in person was a gift: it confirmed I was in good hands. I'm honored that you trusted this French-Canadian food lover to carry out your citrus book project.

Heartfelt thanks to my recipe testers: Isabelle, Marie-Andrée, Elisabeth, Fanny, Marisa, Nicoletta and Loreto, Lindsey, Paula, Carlin, Sarah, Tania, Brona, Sabrina, and Kelly. Your honest and enthusiastic feedback was key to bringing this book as close to perfection as it could be.

An additional thank you to my pro recipe tester, chemist-turned-baker Janice Lawandi, for helping me tweak my dessert recipes. Your knowledge and tips not only made the book better but allowed me to learn new things along the way.

Thank you to my close friends, who were so unbelievably supportive and understanding as I momentarily disappeared from their life while writing this book. Thanks for helping us empty the fridge and freezer when we needed it, too!

Thank you to my parents, Jean-Luc and Réjeane, for always believing in me, no matter what. Mom, it was lovely to have you as an assistant when I was in the weeds testing the recipes. Dad, I appreciated your dishwashing stints, too!

Thank you to the talented photographer who shot this book, Catherine Côté. Catherine, I feel like we still have so much work to do together. We're just getting started!

Last but not least, I'll forever be grateful for the unconditional love and support of the guy who's been sharing my life for over 15 years. Eric, you're the kindest, most generous person I know. You help me become a better person, every day. And kisses to Jules, my son, the light of my life. I'm addicted to seeing your happy, grateful face as you enjoy the food I prepare for you. I look forward to cooking and baking with you for many years to come.

introduction

Ingredients, tools, and techniques

I LIVE IN A NORTHERN CITY where winters are cold and snowy and long–very long. Every year, at the start of the white-clad season, I eagerly survey the arrival of seasonal citrus fruits, which I then rely on to brighten my days. The simple acts of peeling a clementine or shaking a zesty cocktail will unfailingly lift my mood and keep me going.

I can trace the birth of my love for citrus to lemon meringue pie, which is one of the first desserts I started fully making on my own. It was not the typical super-sweet kids' treat, and I remember how sophisticated it felt to bite into that tart yellow filling. Licking the bowl of fluffy meringue also made me feel ridiculously happy, and it still does to this day.

Later in life, I grew an inexhaustible passion for food that would fuel all my projects, both professional and personal. I cooked and baked on a daily basis. When friends asked for my recipes, they would remark that my food had a spark that made it stand out. After a while, I realized that the spark came from citrus fruits: I used lots of lemons, limes, and oranges, both in savory and sweet dishes. If a recipe included citrus juice or zest, I'd double or triple the amounts requested. That simple tweak made the result exciting and bright. Citrus fruits were my secret tools, and my fascination with them only kept on growing.

It feels natural, then, that my first cookbook would be about citrus fruits. I've gathered easy savory and sweet recipes that put citrus fruits front and center. Not just a drizzle of juice here or a grating of zest there. Rather, these are full-on, citrus-forward recipes that prove that lemons, limes, oranges, and their cousins can play a starring role rather than a supporting one.

Citrus fruits are incredibly versatile, and I believe they should occupy a year-round prime spot in your cooking. I hope my recipes encourage you to fill up your kitchen with bright yellow, green, and orange fruits. If you do, your cooking will never be dull again.

For additional information and recipes, visit my blog FoodNouveau.com.

CITRUS FRUITS

Most of the recipes in this book use citrus fruits you can readily find in supermarkets. Some dishes call for specific varieties, such as Meyer lemons or Key limes, or specialty products, such as orange blossom water, but if you can't find those, I provide substitution recommendations. There exists an incredible number of citrus fruit varieties, but my goal was not to send you on a quest to find rare ingredients. Rather, I want to enable you to make all of this book's recipes year-round.

Organic citrus fruits can be expensive, but I strongly encourage you to buy them for recipes that use whole fruit, or a significant quantity of zest or peel. Organic citrus fruits are untreated and unwaxed, which makes them tastier and safer to eat. If you choose regular fruits, make sure to scrub them thoroughly to remove pesticides and wax before using.

It's useful to know how much juice and zest an average citrus fruit produces. The amount can vary widely according to the season and the fruit's freshness and origin. For that reason, recipes feature both the volume quantity and the approximate number of citrus fruits required. For your general reference:

1 average lemon = $^1/_4$ cup juice = 1 tablespoon zest

1 average lime = 2 tablespoons juice = 2 teaspoons zest

1 average orange = $^1/_2$ cup juice = 2 tablespoons zest

1 average mandarin = $^1/_4$ cup juice = 1 tablespoon zest

1 average clementine = 2 tablespoons juice = 2 teaspoons zest

1 average grapefruit = 1 cup juice = $^1/_4$ cup zest

SALT

My recipes all use fine kosher salt, which has a much softer and subtle flavor than regular table salt. The brand I've been using for years is Diamond Crystal, but there are several other brands on the market. If you can't find kosher salt, you can substitute fine sea salt.

As a garnish, I like to use coarse sea salt or sea salt flakes, such as Fleur de Sel de Guérande and Maldon.

SUGAR

I only use organic unrefined cane sugar in desserts. I find it has a mellower flavor and contributes to the taste of a dish. The recipes in this book call for "granulated sugar" for the sake of simplicity, but you can use unrefined cane sugar or regular granulated white sugar interchangeably.

EGGS

All recipes use large eggs.

OLIVE OIL

All recipes use extra virgin olive oil. In my kitchen, I keep two varieties: one with a smoother taste that I use for cooking, and another with a more assertive, peppery taste that I add to dressings or use as a finishing touch. If you want to keep only one bottle of olive oil, go for a smooth-tasting one as it's the most versatile. Buy the best quality you can afford.

TOOLS OF THE CITRUS TRADE

If you like to cook and bake, I'm sure your kitchen is already equipped with the tools you'll need to make the recipes included in this book. Here, I'll only say a few words about the tools that make a difference when it comes to preparing citrus fruits.

SHARP KNIFE Your quintessential ally for all kitchen tasks is especially handy when it comes to peeling and segmenting citrus fruits, but a top-quality knife will only be useful if it stays sharp. I encourage you to invest in a sharpener.

GRATERS A Microplane rasp grater (or zester) is the citrus fruit lover's best friend. It allows you to effortlessly zest the colorful outer skin of the fruit, leaving all bitter white pith behind.

I also very frequently use a second type of grater: the one with five tiny, sharp holes that dig into the skin, leaving ridges behind. Such graters have rounded handles for a better grip. They're usually cheap; you may even find them at the dollar store. This type of zester will help you prepare my Small Batch Citrus Marmalade (page 21) in a cinch. It's also helpful to produce curly strips of zests you can use to garnish dishes.

If you don't have a grater, a sharp vegetable peeler is another excellent tool to zest citrus fruits. If you only apply gentle pressure, you will quickly collect just the colored peel of the fruit. You can then julienne the peel into thin strips to make Candied Citrus Peel (page 12), marmalade, or to decorate finished dishes.

JUICERS No need to invest in an electric juicer, but a sturdy manual juicer will come in handy for squeezing and pressing citrus juice. I use a simple wooden reamer: it's cheap, easy to clean, and virtually indestructible. Note that you'll need to strain the juice to remove bits of flesh or seeds before measuring it. You can also combine this two-step process by using a manual citrus press, which handily squeezes out the juice and retains the seeds in a single movement.

STAINLESS STEEL WHISK If you're a serious citrus lover, you should invest in a stainless steel whisk. Cheaper whisks are made of alloys that can react to the acidity of citrus juice, leaving a metallic taste behind.

The recipes in this book use a few different techniques to prepare citrus fruits. They may seem tricky to achieve at first, but you'll quickly get better with practice. Always make sure to use a sharp knife: this not only makes your work easier but much safer too.

KEY TECHNIQUES

ZESTING

If a recipe requires finely grated zest, it means you should use a Microplane to collect the zest.

If the recipe requires strips of zest, use a vegetable peeler to first collect the peel and then julienne into thin strips. Alternatively, use a round-handled zester to julienne the peel of whole fruits in no time.

PEELING, SLICING, AND SEGMENTING

Unless the recipe states otherwise, you can assume all citrus fruits need to be peeled, and peeling a citrus fruit for use in a recipe goes beyond simply taking the skin off with your fingers.

PEELING First cut off both the top and bottom of the fruit. Stand the fruit on either of the flat ends. Run a very sharp knife along the fruit from top to bottom, removing the skin and pith, leaving the flesh bare. Rotate the fruit and repeat.

From here, you can either slice the fruit or segment it.

SLICING Turn the peeled fruit on its side and slice it into rounds. This is an easy way to enjoy the flesh of a citrus fruit. I only ever segment fruits when I prepare food for company. I find citrus slices to be just as enjoyable both texture- and taste-wise, but slices are much quicker to prepare, and there's less waste.

SEGMENTING Citrus fruit segments are also called supremes. To collect segments, take the peeled fruit in one hand, and run a sharp knife alongside the membranes, leaving entirely bare pieces of fruit behind. You should make sure to do this over a bowl and squeeze the remaining membrane to catch all dripping juices. You may not need to use that juice in the recipe, but you definitely shouldn't throw it away! Save it for your next smoothie or cocktail.

basics

I'VE ALWAYS FOUND the quickest way to a good meal is a handful of reliable, flavorful condiments. When it comes to citrus fruit confections, homemade is hard to beat: no store-bought dressing or curd will taste better than the ones you just made with freshly zested and squeezed fruits. The basic recipes included in this chapter are used throughout the book. Keep jars of them in the fridge, and you'll always be mere steps away from a delicious citrus-infused dish.

- 4 lemons, 6 limes, 3 oranges, or 1 grapefruit
- 1 cup water
- 1 cup granulated sugar
- $1/4$ cup honey or pure maple syrup
- 1 teaspoon pure vanilla extract

I use candied peels in many ways, both in savory and sweet recipes, so I keep jars of each variety at the back of the fridge. Use a vegetable peeler to remove the peel from the fruit as it excludes all of the white, bitter pith.

PREPARATION TIME: 20 MINUTES | MAKES ABOUT 1 CUP PEELS AND SYRUP

candied citrus peel

Using a vegetable peeler, peel the fruits, keeping only the colored outer layer; remove any white pith from underneath the peel. Slice each piece of peel into $1/4$-inch-wide strips. Measure out $3/4$ cup strips for a batch of candied peels. Juice the peeled fruits until you have $1/2$ cup juice; set aside.

Bring a saucepan of water to a boil. Add the peels and simmer for 5 minutes. Drain the peels, return to the saucepan, refill with water, and bring to a boil again. Simmer for 5 minutes, and then drain and rinse under cold water. Reserve.

In another saucepan, stir together the water, sugar, juice, honey, and vanilla; bring to a boil. Continue boiling until the sugar is completely dissolved, about 1 minute. Reduce heat to medium-low, add the blanched peels and simmer, uncovered, for 20-25 minutes, or until the syrup has thickened and the peel is translucent. Remove from the heat, cover the saucepan, and let cool to room temperature. Transfer to an airtight jar and refrigerate for up to 1 month.

Use the candied peel in syrup, or strain and dip it in sugar or melted chocolate for an extra-special treat.

Preserved lemons have an intriguing salty, umami-filled flavor that instantly adds depth and complexity to dishes both savory and sweet. A little goes a long way, so I've come up with a small-batch recipe that won't bulk up your fridge. My technique, inspired by Rolf and Daughters chef Philip Krajeck, uses lemon wedges instead of whole fruits, which speeds up the pickling process, leaving you just a week away from the finished product.

PREPARATION TIME: 25 MINUTES | MAKES 1 (1-QUART) JAR

preserved lemons

5 lemons (preferably organic)

$1/4$ cup salt

1 teaspoon granulated sugar

$1/2$ teaspoon crushed coriander seeds

$1/2$ teaspoon crushed black pepper

$1/4$ teaspoon turmeric

1 bay leaf

Bring a small saucepan of water to a boil, and then add 3 whole lemons. Boil until soft, about 10 minutes. Reserve $1/2$ cup of the cooking liquid, and then transfer the lemons to a bowl of ice water. Let cool completely (discard remaining cooking liquid).

While the lemons are cooling, squeeze the remaining lemons, producing $1/2$ cup juice. Place juice in the saucepan and add the reserved cooking water, salt, sugar, coriander, pepper, and turmeric.

Cut each boiled lemon into 8 wedges. Heat the lemon juice mixture just to a simmer. Spoon some of the liquid into the bottom of an airtight 1-quart jar. Add a layer of the lemon wedges, and then spoon more of the liquid over the top. Add another layer of lemons, pressing down as you do. Repeat the liquid/lemon layers until you've used up the ingredients and the jar is full. Slide in the bay leaf. Close the jar and refrigerate.

The preserved lemons are ready to use after 1 week, though the flavor will keep developing beyond that. The lemons will keep, refrigerated, for up to 6 months.

EVERYDAY CITRUS DRESSING

1/4 cup freshly squeezed citrus juice (lemon, lime, orange, mandarin, or grapefruit)

1/4 cup extra virgin olive oil

2 tablespoons white balsamic vinegar or white wine vinegar

1 tablespoon finely grated citrus zest (lemon, lime, orange, mandarin, or grapefruit)

1 tablespoon minced shallot

1 teaspoon Dijon mustard

1/2 teaspoon kosher salt

Freshly ground black pepper, to taste

1 teaspoon ground turmeric (optional)

CREAMY ORANGE TAHINI DRESSING

1/4 cup coconut milk

1/4 cup tahini

2 tablespoons orange juice (about 1/2 orange)

2 tablespoons rice vinegar

1 teaspoon honey

1 teaspoon finely grated orange zest (about 1/2 orange)

1/2 teaspoon kosher salt

Freshly ground black pepper, to taste

Making these dressings only takes minutes, and they keep refrigerated for up to 2 weeks. I've developed the habit of making a new batch of each one as soon as I empty a jar, which ensures they're always at the ready when I need them. These dressings are used in many of this book's recipes, so you'll want to stock up.

PREPARATION TIME: 10 MINUTES (EACH)

citrus dressings

EVERYDAY CITRUS DRESSING | MAKES 1/2 CUP

Add all the ingredients to an airtight jar. Close the jar and shake vigorously. Taste and adjust seasoning if needed. Keep refrigerated.

CREAMY ORANGE TAHINI DRESSING | MAKES 1 CUP

Add all the ingredients to an airtight jar. Close the jar and shake vigorously. Taste and adjust seasoning if needed. Keep refrigerated.

Hummus has become a staple in many homes. Grabbing a tub at the grocery store may seem like the easiest path to the delicious chickpea spread, but if you have a food processor, making it at home is super quick (and it tastes better, too). This citrusy version can be used just as you would plain hummus, and you can even turn it into a dressing.

PREPARATION TIME: 10 MINUTES | MAKES 2 CUPS

citrus hummus

Add all the ingredients to the bowl of a food processor. Process until smooth and creamy. If the hummus seems thick, you can thin it with a bit of water until you reach the desired consistency. Taste and adjust seasoning as needed. Store in an airtight container in the refrigerator for up to 1 week.

VARIATION: To transform into a dressing, whisk $1/2$ cup hummus with 2 tablespoons orange juice, 2 tablespoons water, and 1 tablespoon lemon juice. Taste and adjust seasoning as needed.

1 (19-ounce) can chickpeas, rinsed and thoroughly dried

$1/4$ cup freshly squeezed orange juice (about $1/2$ orange)

$1/4$ cup freshly squeezed lemon juice (about 1 lemon)

2 tablespoons extra virgin olive oil

2 tablespoons tahini

1 tablespoon finely chopped preserved lemon rind, pulp discarded (optional, see page 15)

1 tablespoon finely grated orange zest (about $1/2$ orange)

1 teaspoon finely grated lemon zest (about $1/2$ lemon)

1 clove garlic, peeled

1 teaspoon kosher salt

Freshly ground black pepper, to taste

1 tablespoon cornstarch

1 tablespoon water

$^1/_2$ cup freshly squeezed,
strained citrus juice (see
below for fruit quantity)

$^1/_4$ to $^1/_2$ cup granulated sugar
(see below)

2 eggs

$^1/_3$ cup heavy cream or soy cream

APPROXIMATE FRUIT JUICE
TO SUGAR RATIO

1 grapefruit, 4 lemons, 6 limes,
or 18–24 Key limes: $^1/_2$ cup
sugar

6 Meyer lemons: $^1/_3$ cup sugar

3 oranges (blood or regular) or 8
clementines: $^1/_4$ cup sugar

$^1/_2$ cup bottled yuzu juice:
$^1/_2$ cup sugar

I have long used lemon curd as a frosting, filling, and spread. Over the years, my passion for curd has widened to include all citrus varieties: each fruit brings its own personality and purpose to the condiment. I developed this butterless recipe to allow me to indulge with abandon–I'm lactose intolerant–but I've grown to like it even better than the original.

PREPARATION TIME: 20 MINUTES | MAKES ABOUT 12 OUNCES

citrus curd

In a small bowl, whisk the cornstarch with the water. Set aside.

In a saucepan over medium heat, whisk the juice and sugar together until sugar is completely dissolved and bubbly around the edges (no need to boil). Remove from the heat.

In a small bowl, whisk the eggs together, and gradually pour the warm syrup into the eggs, whisking constantly to incorporate. Pour the mixture back into the saucepan and return to medium heat. Add the cornstarch mixture and whisk to incorporate. Continue whisking until the mixture is thick like a soft pudding, about 3 minutes, whisking constantly so the mixture doesn't stick to the bottom of the pan. Remove from heat. Whisk in the cream. Transfer to an airtight jar and refrigerate until completely cold. The curd will keep for up to 1 week.

I have marmalade for breakfast every morning, but I've only recently started to make my own. My secret shortcut for making it is to completely exclude the white pith, which avoids several blanching steps that aim at eliminating the pith's bitter taste. This marmalade isn't fully set; rather, it is slightly runny–perfect for spreading on toast or croissants, or incorporating in a sauce.

PREPARATION TIME: 1 HOUR | MAKES ABOUT 2 CUPS

small-batch citrus marmalade

1 lemon

3 blood or regular oranges, 6 to 8 clementines, or 2 pink grapefruits

2 cups granulated sugar

1 cup water

1 tablespoon pure vanilla extract, or $1/2$ vanilla bean, seeds scraped

Scrub the fruits clean and dry thoroughly. Using a vegetable peeler, peel the fruits, keeping only the colored outer layer; remove any white pith from underneath the peel. Slice the peel into $1/4$-inch-wide strips and transfer to a measuring cup. Using a sharp knife, cut the white pith off the fruits. Chop up the flesh, removing any seeds and white core as you go. You need 2 cups total of combined zest and chopped flesh. TIP I recommend zesting and chopping the fruits one at a time, starting with the lemon, so you can stop zesting and chopping as soon as you reach 2 cups total.

Transfer the zest and flesh to a large saucepan; stir in the water, sugar, and vanilla. Bring to a full boil then lower the heat to simmer for 45 minutes to 1 hour, or until the marmalade is thick and syrupy.

Transfer the marmalade to airtight jars and let cool to room temperature. Refrigerate for up to 1 month.

lemon

POSSIBLY THE BEST KNOWN and most used of all citrus fruits, lemon is the gateway to a world of deliciously bold flavors. There's no need to use a lot to make a big difference: a simple drizzle of lemon juice can completely change the profile of a recipe. Lemon awakens the drowsiest of flavors and perfectly balances out overly rich or sweet dishes. Keep a bag of fresh lemons in the fridge and your cooking will never be dull.

1 (15.5-ounce) can chickpeas, drained, rinsed, and patted dry

$1/2$ head cauliflower, chopped into small florets

1 lemon, cut into 8 wedges

3 cloves garlic, unpeeled

2 tablespoons extra virgin olive oil

2 teaspoons crushed red pepper

1 teaspoon kosher salt

1 tablespoon finely grated lemon zest (about 1 lemon)

1 tablespoon toasted sesame seeds

1 tablespoon fresh thyme leaves

TO SERVE

1 cup Citrus Hummus (page 17) or store-bought plain hummus

24 mini pita breads

The heart of this recipe is a zesty salad, and the best thing about it is its versatility. Here, we spoon it over hummus to serve as a bite, but you can also stuff it in a pita along with crunchy lettuce to make a delicious lunch. It's equally enjoyable warm or cold.

PREPARATION TIME: 45 MINUTES | MAKES 24 BITES

spicy roasted lemon, cauliflower, and chickpea bites

Preheat oven to 450°F. Line a baking sheet with parchment paper.

In a large bowl, add the chickpeas, cauliflower, lemon, and garlic. Drizzle with the olive oil, and then add the red pepper and salt. Toss to coat. Spread mixture evenly over the baking sheet and roast for 20 minutes, until browned in bits. Remove from the oven and let cool slightly.

Press the roasted lemon slices to release their juice onto the cauliflower and chickpea mixture (discard the wedges). Press the roasted garlic cloves to release the tender flesh (discard the peels). Add the lemon zest, sesame seeds, and thyme. Toss and transfer to a serving bowl.

To serve, smear about 2 teaspoons hummus on each pita bread, and then top with some of the roasted chickpea salad.

The idea for these cakes came to me while I was enjoying a slice of sweet lemon and olive oil cake. Wouldn't a savory version of the recipe be great as an appetizer? Serve these elegant bite-size cakes with smoked salmon, hearty soups, dips, cheeses, or cured meats.

PREPARATION TIME: 30 MINUTES | MAKES 24 MINI CAKES

savory lemon and olive oil cakes

Preheat oven to 350°F. Grease a 24-cup mini muffin pan with cooking spray.

In a large mixing bowl, whisk together the flour, baking powder, pepper, baking soda, and salt. In a second bowl, whisk the eggs, oil, lemon zest, and juice. Pour the oil mixture over the flour mixture. Using a spatula, mix just to combine. Stir in the mix-ins.

Divide batter evenly between muffin cups and bake for about 15 minutes, or until a toothpick inserted in the center of a cake comes out clean.

Serve the cakes warm or at room temperature.

Note: The batter can also be baked in a standard muffin pan or in a 9 x 5-inch loaf pan. Make sure to adjust baking time accordingly: 22-25 minutes for muffins or 50-60 minutes for a loaf.

1 1/2 cups all-purpose flour

1 teaspoon baking powder

1 teaspoon coarsely ground black pepper

1/2 teaspoon baking soda

1/2 teaspoon kosher salt

3 eggs

1/2 cup extra virgin olive oil

1 tablespoon finely grated lemon zest (about 1 lemon)

1/4 cup freshly squeezed and strained lemon juice (about 1 lemon)

MIX-INS (OPTIONAL; CHOOSE ONE OR COMBINE FOR 1/2 CUP TOTAL)

1/4 cup grated Parmesan cheese

1/4 cup chopped pistachios or walnuts

1/4 cup chopped fresh herbs (such as basil, thyme, oregano, or flat-leaf parsley)

1/4 cup finely diced fried pancetta

1/4 cup chopped pitted green or black olives

CHICKEN AND FETA SKEWERS

1 tablespoon finely grated lemon zest (about 1 lemon)

2 tablespoons freshly squeezed lemon juice (about $1/2$ lemon)

1 tablespoon extra virgin olive oil

1 tablespoon chopped fresh cilantro

1 teaspoon curry powder

$1/2$ teaspoon ground cumin

1 clove garlic, minced

$1/4$ teaspoon kosher salt

Freshly ground black pepper, to taste

4 chicken breasts (about 2 pounds), cut into 1-inch cubes

8 (1-inch) cubes feta cheese (about 6 ounces)

MINT CUCUMBER SALAD

6 Lebanese cucumbers, unpeeled, cut into rounds

2 cups halved cherry tomatoes

$1/4$ cup chopped fresh mint leaves

$1/4$ cup minced red onion

Everyday Citrus Dressing (lemon variation page 16), to taste

Sea salt flakes and freshly ground black pepper, to taste

This recipe is one of my go-to weeknight meals: throw the chicken, feta, and marinade ingredients together in the morning, and come back to a flavorful dinner that cooks in less than 10 minutes. The cucumber salad makes it a complete meal in no time.

PREPARATION TIME: 45 MINUTES PLUS AT LEAST 1 HOUR FOR MARINATING | MAKES 8 (6-INCH) SKEWERS

curried chicken and feta skewers with mint cucumber salad

CHICKEN AND FETA SKEWERS In a large ziplock bag, add all the marinade ingredients and mix to combine. Add the chicken and feta cubes, mix to coat with marinade, seal, and refrigerate for 1 hour to overnight.

Position a rack in the upper third of the oven, and preheat the broiler on high. Line a baking sheet with aluminum foil and lightly coat with oil.

Thread the marinated chicken and feta onto 8 (6-inch) skewers. Set the skewers on the baking sheet. Broil for 3-4 minutes on each side, or until the chicken is cooked through. Let rest while you assemble the salad.

MINT CUCUMBER SALAD In a salad bowl, combine the cucumbers, tomatoes, mint, and onion. Toss with the dressing and season with salt and pepper. Serve the skewers warm with salad on the side.

A riff on a classic Greek dish called *avgolemono*, this soup is quick and easy to make. The broth is silky but light, and the full-bodied flavors are incredibly comforting. The paper-thin lemon toppings are a classic way to serve the soup, but you can skip them and just dig in.

PREPARATION TIME: 30 MINUTES | SERVES 4 TO 6

greek lemon and egg soup

In a large saucepan, bring the broth to a boil. Add the rice, lower to a simmer, cover, and cook for 15 minutes.

In a small bowl, whisk the eggs with the lemon juice. Slowly whisk a ladleful of hot broth into the egg mixture to warm it. Whisking constantly, slowly pour the egg mixture back into the saucepan. Cook, whisking constantly, for 2-3 minutes, or until the soup is slightly thickened (do not let it boil, or the eggs might curdle). Season with salt and pepper; stir in the chicken.

Serve garnished with lemon slices and fresh thyme.

6 cups chicken broth

1 cup brown basmati rice or another long-grain rice

3 eggs

1/4 cup freshly squeezed and strained lemon juice (about 1 lemon)

1 teaspoon fresh thyme leaves, or 1/4 teaspoon dried thyme

1/2 teaspoon kosher salt

Freshly ground black pepper, to taste

1 cup shredded or diced cooked chicken

TO SERVE

Paper-thin lemon slices

Fresh thyme leaves

- 1 tablespoon plus $1/2$ teaspoon kosher salt, divided
- 2 lemons, scrubbed clean
- 2 tablespoons extra virgin olive oil, divided
- $1/2$ teaspoon granulated sugar
- 5 cups chicken stock
- 1 tablespoon butter
- 1 fennel bulb, very thinly sliced, fronds reserved for garnish
- $1/4$ teaspoon crushed red pepper
- 10 ounces risotto rice (such as Arborio, baldo, or carnaroli)
- 1 cup dry white wine
- $1/2$ cup grated Parmesan cheese
- Kosher salt and freshly ground black pepper, to taste

If there's a recipe that makes it worth seeking organic lemons, this is it. I borrowed the idea of caramelizing lemon slices from famed cookbook writer Melissa Clark; the process of boiling and frying eliminates any bitterness. The perfect dish for die-hard lemon fans.

PREPARATION TIME: 45 MINUTES | SERVES 4

caramelized lemon and fennel risotto

Fill a saucepan with water, add 1 tablespoon salt, and bring to a boil. Cut the tops and bottoms off the lemons then cut lengthwise into quarters and remove seeds. Thinly slice the lemon wedges into triangles. When the water simmers, add the lemon pieces and blanch for 2 minutes. Drain and dry on paper towels.

In a large, shallow skillet, heat 1 tablespoon olive oil over high heat. When shimmering, add the lemon pieces and sprinkle with $1/2$ teaspoon salt and sugar. Sauté until the lemons are caramelized, about 5 minutes. Transfer to a plate and set aside. Do not rinse the skillet.

Pour the chicken stock into a saucepan and bring to a simmer. Cover and turn the heat to low just to keep warm.

In the skillet you used to fry the lemons, melt the butter with the remaining olive oil over medium-low heat. Add half of the fennel slices and the red pepper. and sauté for 3 minutes. Add the rice and stir for 2 minutes. Add the wine and simmer until absorbed.

Add 1 ladleful chicken broth and stir until almost completely absorbed. Continue adding broth, 1 ladleful at a time, allowing broth to be absorbed before adding more. When there are about 2 ladlefuls of broth left, stir in the remaining fennel. Keep stirring and adding broth until the rice is al dente, and the mixture is creamy but not stiff.

Stir the Parmesan into the risotto until melted and creamy. Stir in the caramelized lemon pieces, season with salt and pepper, garnish with fennel fronds, and serve immediately.

CRUST

³/₄ cup all-purpose flour

³/₄ cup toasted unsweetened
 shredded coconut

¹/₃ cup powdered sugar

1 tablespoon cornstarch

¹/₄ teaspoon kosher salt

¹/₄ cup melted coconut oil

FILLING

³/₄ cup granulated sugar

3 tablespoons cornstarch

Pinch of kosher salt

3 large eggs

2 teaspoons finely grated lemon
 zest (about 1 lemon)

³/₄ cup freshly squeezed lemon
 juice (about 3 lemons)

TO SERVE

Powdered sugar

Toasted unsweetened shredded
 coconut

In this delicious, dairy-free variation of a timeless classic, coconut adds an exotic twist: toasted shredded coconut gives a nice crunch to the crust while the rich aroma of coconut oil rounds off the tartness of lemon.

PREPARATION TIME: 1 HOUR PLUS ABOUT 2 HOURS 30 MINUTES FOR COOLING | MAKES 12 BARS

coconut lemon bars

Preheat oven to 350°F. Grease an 8-inch square baking pan and line with parchment paper, letting it overhang on two sides (this will make it easier to pull the squares out later).

CRUST In a medium bowl, combine the flour, coconut, powdered sugar, cornstarch, and salt. Stir the oil into the flour mixture until fully incorporated. Place the dough into the prepared pan, and firmly press down all the way to the sides. Bake the crust until it just starts to brown around the edges, 15–20 minutes.

FILLING In a medium bowl, whisk the sugar, cornstarch, and salt until well combined. Add the eggs, one at a time, whisking until each one is fully incorporated before adding the next. Add the lemon zest and juice; whisk until the mixture is completely smooth.

Pour the filling over the hot crust. Bake until the filling is just set, 15–18 minutes. The filling should start to turn golden around the edges, and the center should be a bit jiggly (it will firm up as it cools). Let the squares cool completely to room temperature, and then refrigerate for 2 hours before cutting.

Just before serving, dust the bars with powdered sugar and garnish with coconut.

Here's a quick, no-bake treat for hot summer nights. Meyer lemons are a cross between Mandarin oranges and lemons, which makes them sweeter than the regular variety. Their mellow flavor complements fresh seasonal berries, but you can also use any other citrus curd in this recipe.

PREPARATION TIME: 25 MINUTES | SERVES 6

meyer lemon mousse with honey-basil berries

2 cups mixed fresh berries (such as blackberries, raspberries, and strawberries)

2 tablespoons honey

10 medium fresh basil leaves, minced

$^3/_4$ cup whipping cream

1 batch Meyer lemon curd (page 18, about 12 ounces)

In a bowl, toss the berries with the honey and basil. Let rest at room temperature for 15 minutes.

In a large bowl, beat the whipping cream until soft peaks form. Add the lemon curd and, using a spatula, fold just to incorporate.

Divide the mousse between 6 serving glasses, and then top with honey-basil berries. Serve, or refrigerate for up to 6 hours.

CRÊPES

2 cups all-purpose flour

$1/4$ cup granulated sugar

6 eggs

1 cup milk

1 cup water

Canola oil, for cooking

MASCARPONE FILLING

1 cup (8 ounces) mascarpone cheese

$1/2$ cup whipping cream

$1/4$ cup granulated sugar

1 teaspoon pure vanilla extract

LEMON FILLING

1 batch lemon curd (page 18, about 12 ounces)

TO SERVE

Candied lemon peel (see page 12)

This spectacular dessert will impress and delight your guests, but you'll appreciate how manageable it is to make. You can prepare the crêpes days in advance, and even freeze the assembled cake up to a week ahead of when you need it. Make sure to use a sharp knife to cut the cake neatly.

PREPARATION TIME: 1 HOUR 10 MINUTES PLUS AT LEAST 1 HOUR FOR REFRIGERATION | SERVES 8

mile-high lemon and mascarpone crêpe cake

CRÊPES: In a blender or food processor, combine the flour, sugar, eggs, milk, and water until smooth, scraping the sides once or twice. Transfer to an airtight container and refrigerate for at least 30 minutes, or overnight.

Lightly coat an 8-inch nonstick skillet with oil, and then place over medium heat. Pour $1/4$ cup batter into the pan then immediately swirl so the batter covers the whole bottom of the skillet. Cook until the underside of the crêpe is lightly browned, about 1 minute. Flip the crêpe and cook until the second side is lightly browned, about 30 seconds. Slide onto a plate. Repeat to make all crêpes, stacking them on a plate as you go (you should end up with about 24 crêpes total). Let the crêpes cool completely, and then cover with plastic wrap and refrigerate until needed.

MASCARPONE FILLING: In a large mixing bowl, whip the mascarpone cheese, whipping cream, sugar, and vanilla until soft peaks form.

TO ASSEMBLE: Place 1 crêpe on a flat serving dish. Spread with a thin layer of lemon curd. Top with a second crêpe. Spread with a thin layer of mascarpone filling. Continue layering crêpes, curd, and mascarpone filling until only 1 crepe remains (you should have some mascarpone filling leftover). End this layering process with the final crêpe, cover the cake with plastic wrap, and refrigerate until firm, about 1 hour. You can also loosely cover the assembled cake with plastic wrap and freeze for up to 1 week. Transfer to the fridge overnight to defrost.

Right before serving, top the cake with the remaining mascarpone filling, and then garnish with the candied lemon peel.

This cocktail is my long-time favorite drink. A variation on the Penicillin cocktail, created by New York City mixologist Sam Ross, it's tart and refreshing and intriguingly smoky. If you don't have maple syrup on hand, you can substitute honey.

PREPARATION TIME: 5 MINUTES | MAKES 1 COCKTAIL

scotch, ginger, and lemon cocktail

Add both Scotches, the ginger, lemon juice, and syrup to a cocktail shaker; top with 4 ice cubes. Shake until the cocktail is icy cold, about 20 seconds.

Strain into a glass filled with ice cubes. Top with a splash of soda and garnish with a slice of ginger. Enjoy right away.

$1^1/_2$ ounces blended Scotch

$^1/_2$ ounce single-malt Scotch (choose a smoky variety, such as those from Islay)

3 thin slices fresh ginger, plus more for garnish

1 ounce lemon juice

$^1/_2$ ounce pure maple syrup

Ice cubes

Soda or sparkling water

lime

A UBIQUITOUS INGREDIENT in so many cuisines around the world, I find lime to be incredibly versatile. The fruit's sharp, summery flavor brightens dishes and lends itself to a variety of both savory and sweet dishes. When buying limes, look for the ones with supple skin: they're the juiciest. If you can get your hands on a bag of Key limes, make sure to bring it home. They're a lot of work to juice, but they make up for your effort with their lovely floral, complex flavor.

CORN SALSA

2 cups fresh corn kernels

2 tablespoons extra virgin olive oil

2 tablespoons chopped fresh cilantro

1 lime, peeled and finely diced

1 teaspoon honey

$1/2$ teaspoon ground cumin

$1/2$ teaspoon smoked sea salt or sea salt flakes

Freshly ground black pepper, to taste

CRAB CAKES

1 pound crabmeat, fresh or defrosted, patted dry

1 cup panko

$1/4$ cup chopped fresh cilantro

2 green onions, minced

2 tablespoons finely chopped jalapeño pepper (about 1 pepper)

$1/4$ cup freshly squeezed lime juice (about 2 limes)

1 teaspoon finely grated lime zest (about $1/2$ lime)

2 eggs

1 clove garlic, minced

$1/2$ teaspoon kosher salt

These fresh and summery crab cakes are delicious hot, but also cold, making them perfect for a picnic. You can use any crab variety, fresh or frozen, but the salsa is exceptionally better if you can use fresh, seasonal corn.

PREPARATION TIME: 35 MINUTES | MAKES 8 CRAB CAKES

jalapeño crab cakes with corn salsa

Preheat oven to 425°F. Line a baking sheet with parchment paper.

CORN SALSA Bring a small pot of salted water to a boil. Add the corn kernels and blanch for 1 minute. Drain and rinse under cold water. Pat kernels dry and transfer to a bowl. Add the olive oil, cilantro, lime, honey, and cumin; toss to combine. Season with salt and pepper. Set aside.

CRAB CAKES In a large mixing bowl, combine all the ingredients. Using an ice cream scoop or your hands, create patties of about $1/4$ cup mixture each. Place the patties on the prepared baking sheet. Bake for 7 minutes, flip the patties, and then bake for another 7 minutes, or until golden and crisp.

Serve the crab cakes warm, topped with the corn salsa.

Ceviche is such a quick dish to prepare, yet it delivers an impressive depth of flavor. In this version, the rich coconut milk complements the bright taste of lime and spicy touch of ginger and jalapeño, creating a dish that's elegant enough to be served on a special night.

PREPARATION TIME: 15 MINUTES PLUS AT LEAST 30 MINUTES FOR MARINATING | SERVES 4

lime, ginger, and coconut ceviche

Place a glass or stainless steel bowl over a larger bowl filled with ice. Set aside.

Using a very sharp knife, cut the fish into $3/4$-inch cubes. Transfer to the bowl set over ice. Add the lime juice, coconut milk, garlic, jalapeño pepper, and ginger and stir with a spoon to distribute the flavorings and coat the fish. Sprinkle with the salt and stir again. Cover the bowl with plastic wrap and refrigerate for 30 minutes to an hour.

To serve, divide the marinated fish between 4 serving plates. Sprinkle each serving with green onion, peanuts, and cilantro. Serve immediately.

1 pound firm white fish fillets (such as sea bass, grouper, or flounder)

$1/4$ cup freshly squeezed lime juice (about 2 limes)

$1/4$ cup coconut milk

1 clove garlic, minced

1 teaspoon minced jalapeño pepper (about $1/2$ pepper)

$1/2$ teaspoon grated fresh ginger

1 teaspoon sea salt flakes

TO SERVE

1 green onion, minced (green part only)

Chopped salted peanuts

Fresh cilantro leaves

1 tablespoon extra virgin olive oil

1 small onion, halved and thinly sliced

1 clove garlic, minced

2 tablespoons Thai red curry paste

2 teaspoons grated fresh ginger

2 cups vegetable stock

1 (13.5-ounce) can coconut milk

1 cup red lentils, rinsed

1/4 cup freshly squeezed lime juice (about 2 limes)

1/2 pound peeled and deveined medium shrimp (31 to 40 count)

1/2 teaspoon kosher salt

TO SERVE

Fresh cilantro leaves

This hearty soup is incredibly flavorful and comes together in minutes. Like most curried dishes, the aromas in this soup continue to develop as it rests, so you can make it in advance and reheat just before serving.

PREPARATION TIME: 30 MINUTES | SERVES 4

curried coconut, lentil, and shrimp soup

In a medium saucepan, heat the olive oil over medium heat until shimmering. Add the onion and sauté until soft, about 3 minutes. Add the garlic, curry paste, and ginger; stir until fragrant, about 1 minute. Add the vegetable stock, coconut milk, and lentils. Bring to a boil, and then reduce heat and simmer for 10 minutes. Add the lime juice and shrimp; simmer until the shrimp is just cooked through, about 5 minutes. Season with salt. Divide between 4 serving bowls, garnish each portion with cilantro, and serve.

SEARED BEEF

1/4 cup freshly squeezed lime juice (about 2 limes)

1/4 cup extra virgin olive oil

2 cloves garlic, minced

1 teaspoon Mexican chili powder*

1 teaspoon kosher salt

Freshly ground black pepper, to taste

1 pound flank steak

LIME-ROASTED VEGETABLES

1 sweet potato, peeled and diced (about 2 cups)

2 bell peppers (red, yellow, or orange), cored and diced (about 2 cups)

1 small red onion, sliced

1 lime, sliced lengthwise into 8 wedges

2 tablespoons extra virgin olive oil

1 teaspoon ground cumin

1 teaspoon kosher salt

Freshly ground black pepper, to taste

I'm always looking for new ways to incorporate more vegetables into my tacos, and these easy-to-make lime-infused roasted vegetables are a favorite at my house. Swap the beef for chicken breast or thighs for an equally delicious result.

PREPARATION TIME: 50 MINUTES PLUS AT LEAST 30 MINUTES FOR MARINATING | MAKES 8 TACOS

seared beef and lime-roasted vegetable tacos

SEARED BEEF In a ziplock bag, combine the lime juice, olive oil, garlic, chili powder, salt, and pepper. Add the steak. Marinate at room temperature for 30 minutes, or for several hours to overnight in the fridge. (If you refrigerate the steak, bring it back to room temperature 30 minutes before cooking.)

8 soft corn tortillas

$1/4$ cup Greek yogurt, whisked with 1 tablespoon freshly squeezed lime juice and $1/2$ teaspoon kosher salt

Crumbled feta cheese

Fresh cilantro leaves

Toasted pumpkin seeds

LIME-ROASTED VEGETABLES Preheat oven to 450°F. Line a baking sheet with aluminum foil and lightly coat with oil. In a large bowl, combine the sweet potato, bell peppers, onion, lime, olive oil, cumin, salt, and pepper; toss to coat. Spread vegetables over the baking sheet. Roast for 15 minutes, or until the lime is charred and the vegetables are crisp-tender. Keep the oven on.

Remove the steak from the marinade. Heat an oiled pan over medium-high heat. Sear the steak for 2 minutes on each side then transfer to the oven for 6-8 minutes, until the steak is cooked to medium-rare. Transfer the steak to a cutting board and let rest for 10 minutes. Thinly slice across the grain.

Squeeze the lime wedges over the vegetables and toss to coat. Transfer to a serving bowl. Serve the sliced steak, roasted vegetables, tortillas, and garnishes family style.

* Mexican chili powder is a spice blend that usually includes cumin, paprika, cayenne pepper, oregano, and garlic powder. If you can't find it, substitute a home blend that combines equal parts of the 5 spices.

1 tablespoon extra virgin olive oil

1 medium onion, thinly sliced

2 cloves garlic, minced

3 tablespoons Thai green curry paste

1 (13.5-ounce) can coconut milk

1 cup chicken broth

2 boneless, skinless chicken breasts (about 1 pound)

$1/2$ cup toasted unsweetened shredded coconut

4 cups mixed green vegetables (such as asparagus, zucchini, broccoli, green beans, Brussels sprouts, and green peas), cut into bite-size pieces

1 teaspoon finely grated lime zest (about 1 lime)

$1/4$ cup freshly squeezed lime juice (about 2 limes)

1 teaspoon kosher salt

TO SERVE

Toasted unsweetened shredded coconut

2 green onions, minced

Fresh basil leaves

Steamed basmati rice

I like to make curry year-round using the best and freshest seasonal produce. In this recipe, green veggies ramp up the nutritional value of the dish, while the flavor of coconut milk is emphasized by crunchy toasted coconut flakes.

PREPARATION TIME: 35 MINUTES | SERVES 4

chicken and toasted coconut green curry

In a large pot, heat the olive oil over medium heat until shimmering. Add the onion and sauté for about 3 minutes, until tender. Add the garlic and curry paste, and stir for 1 minute, until fragrant. Add the coconut milk and chicken broth and bring to a boil. Lower the heat, add the chicken and coconut, and simmer for 15 minutes, stirring occasionally, until the chicken is cooked through. Transfer the chicken to a plate. Add the green vegetables to the pot and simmer for 5-7 minutes, until crisp-tender.

While the vegetables are cooking, shred or slice the cooked chicken. When the vegetables are done, add the chicken back to the pot. Stir in the lime zest and juice, and season with salt. Taste and adjust the seasoning as needed.

Serve the curry garnished with shredded coconut, green onions, and fresh basil, with the rice on the side.

I like tabbouleh to pile on textures and flavors: it then becomes a hearty salad you could eat as a main dish if you felt like it. With salty, crunchy, and smoky elements, this nourishing version is downright dreamy served with a runny egg on top.

PREPARATION TIME: 20 MINUTES | SERVES 4

kale, cilantro, and chorizo tabbouleh

Place the couscous in a bowl or a large measuring cup. Bring the vegetable broth to a boil then pour over the couscous. Stir, cover with plastic wrap, and let rest for 10 minutes.

In a large bowl, combine the kale, cilantro, and parsley. Fluff the cooked couscous with a fork, and then add it to the salad (the couscous should still be warm when adding it to the salad). Toss to incorporate the couscous. Drizzle the dressing over the salad and mix well. Add the pumpkin seeds, chorizo, and feta; toss just to combine. Taste and add more dressing or adjust seasoning as needed. Transfer to a serving bowl.

Serve immediately, or refrigerate in an airtight container for up to 1 day.

$1/2$ cup couscous

1 cup vegetable broth or water

2 leaves kale, stemmed and finely chopped (about 2 cups, loosely packed)

$1/2$ cup finely chopped cilantro leaves and stems

$1/2$ cup finely chopped flat-leaf parsley

$1/2$ cup Everyday Citrus Dressing (lime variation, page 16), plus more as needed

$1/4$ cup toasted pumpkin seeds

$1/2$ cup diced dry-cured Spanish chorizo

$1/4$ cup crumbled feta cheese

1 cup whipping cream

1 batch Key lime curd (page 18, about 12 ounces)

1 store-bought angel food cake (about 9 ounces)

7 passion fruits

2 tablespoons orange juice

1 tablespoon honey

4 cups fresh raspberries

TO SERVE

Powdered sugar

Very few desserts offer the same easy-to-impressive ratio as v does. A classic addition to holiday tables, It's also the perfect dessert to serve on a hot summer day–especially when it features exotic passion fruits, aromatic Key limes, and fresh berries.

PREPARATION TIME: 30 MINUTES PLUS 1 HOUR FOR REFRIGERATION | SERVES 8

key lime, passion fruit, and raspberry trifle

In a mixing bowl, whip the cream to soft peaks. Fold in the Key lime curd.

Halve 6 of the passion fruits, and scoop out the pulp into a small bowl. Mix the pulp with the orange juice and honey.

Cut the angel food cake into $1\,^1/_2$-inch cubes.

Lay one-third of the cake cubes in the bottom of a trifle dish or a large glass bowl. Spoon one-third of the passion fruit syrup over the cake. Top with one-third of the Key lime cream, and then sprinkle one-third of the raspberries overtop. Repeat the layers twice, ending with raspberries. Halve the remaining passion fruit, and drizzle its pulp over the trifle.

Refrigerate for 1 hour (the trifle can be refrigerated for up to 1 day before serving). Just before serving, lightly dust with powdered sugar if desired.

Crunchy, buttery, and only slightly sweet, shortbread cookies are a blank canvas I can adapt countless ways. This hazelnut-lime number is a long-time favorite and one of my most requested recipes. If you don't have whole-wheat flour on hand, you can substitute additional white flour.

PREPARATION TIME: 1 HOUR | MAKES ABOUT 20 COOKIES

hazelnut shortbread cookies with lime cream cheese frosting

HAZELNUT COOKIES In a mixing bowl, combine the hazelnuts, white and wheat flours, baking powder, and salt. In another bowl, beat the butter, powdered sugar, and vanilla together until the mixture is fluffy and pale, about 3 minutes. Add the egg yolk and beat well.

Add the flour mixture to the butter mixture, and mix at low speed until the dough is just combined, about 1 minute. Gather the dough together into a ball, split into halves, and then wrap each portion in plastic wrap. Refrigerate for 30 minutes.

Remove the dough from the refrigerator and let rest at room temperature for 15 minutes. Set a rack in the middle of the oven and preheat to 350°F. Line 2 baking sheets with parchment paper.

(continued)

HAZELNUT COOKIES

1 cup ground toasted hazelnuts (3.5 ounces)

$^1/_2$ cup all-purpose flour

$^1/_2$ cup whole-wheat all-purpose flour

$^1/_4$ teaspoon baking powder

$^1/_4$ teaspoon kosher salt

$^1/_2$ cup (4 ounces) unsalted butter, room temperature

$^1/_2$ cup powdered sugar

1 teaspoon pure vanilla extract

1 egg yolk

LIME CREAM CHEESE FROSTING

$^1/_4$ cup (2 ounces) cream cheese, room temperature

2 tablespoons (1 ounce) butter, room temperature

1 teaspoon finely grated lime zest (about $^1/_2$ lime)

2 tablespoons freshly squeezed and strained lime juice (about 1 lime)

1 teaspoon pure vanilla extract

3 cups powdered sugar, sifted

Set a large piece of parchment paper onto a work surface, place the first ball of dough in the center, and then cover with another piece of parchment paper. Roll the dough out to $1/8$ inch thick (the dough may crack during the process; simply pat it back together using your fingers). Using a 2-inch round cookie cutter, cut out as many shapes as possible. Use an offset spatula or a knife to carefully transfer the cookies onto the prepared baking sheets, setting about 1 inch apart to allow for some light spreading. Gather the scraps, reroll, and cut out new shapes, repeating until there is no dough left. Repeat with the second ball of dough.

Bake the first sheet of cookies for 15-20 minutes, rotating the sheet halfway through, until pale golden around the edges. Cool the cookies for a few minutes on the baking sheet, and then transfer to a wire rack to cool completely. Bake the remaining cookies.

LIME CREAM CHEESE FROSTING Beat the cream cheese, butter, lime zest, lime juice, and vanilla extract together. Gradually add in the powdered sugar, beating until creamy and light. Store in an airtight container in the fridge until ready to use.

TO ASSEMBLE Spread a thick layer of frosting on the underside of a cookie. Cover with another cookie, very gently pressing to spread the frosting all the way to the sides of the cookie (shortbread cookies are crumbly, so make sure to proceed with care.) Repeat to assemble all cookies.

Store in an airtight container in the refrigerator. The cookies are best enjoyed within 3 days.

Although it may sound counterintuitive, eating spicy foods in hot weather helps cool you down. I created this summery day drink with that principle in mind. For a festive evening, add your choice of liquor (see note below).

PREPARATION TIME: 30 MINUTES PLUS 1 HOUR FOR REFRIGERATION | MAKES ABOUT 6 CUPS

cayenne limeade

8 limes, scrubbed clean, room temperature

5 cups water, divided

$1/2$ cup honey

$1/2$ cup granulated sugar

$1/4$ teaspoon ground cayenne pepper

TO SERVE

Ice

Fresh basil leaves

Ground cayenne pepper

Using a vegetable peeler or a sharp knife, peel the zest of the limes in $1/2$-inch-thick strips. Roll each lime between your palm and the countertop to soften. Halve and juice the limes (you should end up with about 1 cup juice).

In a saucepan, combine 1 cup water with the honey, sugar, cayenne pepper, and lime zests. Set over medium heat and bring to a simmer. Stir, remove from the heat, cover, and cool to room temperature.

Strain the honey syrup into a large pitcher (discard solids). Add the lime juice and remaining water. Refrigerate for at least 1 hour, or until cold.

To serve, pour over ice. Garnish with fresh basil and a pinch of cayenne pepper, if desired.

Note: To turn this limeade into a refreshing cocktail, combine $1/4$ cup limeade and 1 ounce tequila or rum in an ice-filled shaker. Shake for about 20 seconds, and then strain into an ice-filled glass. Top with sparkling or soda water. Enjoy right away.

orange

ORANGES COME IN MANY shapes and forms, and I believe no one can remain impervious to their charm. Simply peeling an orange infuses the whole room with a sweet aroma that has the power to uplift the gloomiest moods. Sweet Valencia and navel orange varieties are an easy and versatile choice, but in season, make sure to pick up blood oranges: their showstopping color and ever-so-slightly sour taste will wow you and your guests, guaranteed.

- 1 pound peeled and deveined medium shrimp (31 to 40 count)
- $^1/_2$ teaspoon kosher salt
- Freshly ground black pepper, to taste
- 4 links fresh Mexican chorizo
- 2 regular or blood oranges, peeled and sliced (see page 9)
- 2 tablespoons minced fresh chives
- 2 tablespoons minced fresh flat-leaf parsley
- Sea salt flakes, to taste
- $^1/_2$ cup Everyday Citrus Dressing (orange variation, page 16), plus more to taste

TO SERVE

Toasted baguette slices

Tapas dishes are better when shared with friends, and this fresh and hearty summertime appetizer is no exception. Make sure to serve it with fresh crusty bread so you can mop up the delicious dressing.

PREPARATION TIME: 15 MINUTES | SERVES 4

grilled shrimp, chorizo, and orange tapa

Heat grill to medium-high heat and oil the grate, or set an oiled grill pan over medium-high heat. Thread the shrimp onto skewers then season with salt and pepper. Grill the shrimp skewers for 2 minutes on each side, and the chorizo for 5 minutes on each side, or until cooked through. Transfer the skewers to a plate and cool slightly.

Remove the shrimp from the skewers and put into a large mixing bowl. Slice the chorizo into rounds, and add to the bowl. Add the oranges, chives, and parsley; toss to combine. Drizzle with the dressing, and season with sea salt and pepper. Taste and add more dressing, if needed. Transfer to a serving dish and serve with the baguette slices.

A riot of flavor and textures, this colorful salad inevitably creates a wow effect every time I serve it. It's an excellent way to sneak healthy lentils into your diet, though you could substitute chickpeas if you prefer.

PREPARATION TIME: 30 MINUTES PLUS AT LEAST 20 MINUTES FOR COOLING | SERVES 4

roasted sweet potato, lentil, and orange salad

Preheat oven to 400°F. Line a baking sheet with parchment paper.

In a small bowl, combine the sweet potatoes, olive oil, orange zest, salt, cumin, and pepper. Spread potatoes on the baking sheet, making sure to scrape down the bowl over the potatoes so that all the seasoning is used. Roast for 15 minutes, or until the potatoes are golden and tender. If desired, broil for 1 minute to add some char. Let cool completely.

In a large bowl, gently toss together the potatoes, lentils, orange slices, parsley, feta, pomegranate seeds, and pistachios. Drizzle with the dressing and toss to combine. Serve immediately.

1 large sweet potato (about 1 pound), peeled and sliced into $1/4$-inch-thick semicircles

2 tablespoons olive oil

1 tablespoon orange zest (about $1/2$ orange)

$1/2$ teaspoon kosher salt

$1/2$ teaspoon cumin

Freshly ground black pepper, to taste

1 (15-ounce) can lentils, rinsed, drained, and patted dry

2 oranges, peeled and sliced (see page 9)

$1/2$ cup chopped flat-leaf parsley

$1/2$ cup crumbled feta cheese

$1/4$ cup pomegranate seeds (optional)

$1/4$ cup shelled pistachios

Everyday Citrus Dressing (orange and turmeric variation, page 16), to taste

ORANGE AND GINGER PORK SLIDERS

1 pound lean ground pork

$^1/_4$ cup breadcrumbs

2 green onions, minced

2 tablespoons shoyu (Japanese soy sauce)

2 teaspoons grated ginger

1 tablespoon finely grated orange zest (about $^1/_2$ orange)

1 teaspoon sambal oelek

1 teaspoon kosher salt

PEANUT SLAW

2 tablespoons peanut butter

2 tablespoons shoyu (Japanese soy sauce)

1 tablespoon finely grated orange zest (about $^1/_2$ orange)

1 tablespoon pure maple syrup or honey

1 tablespoon rice vinegar

1 clove garlic, minced

3 cups coleslaw mix (or a mix of shredded cabbage and carrot)

2 green onions, minced

$^1/_2$ cup chopped salted peanuts

TO SERVE

12 slider buns

Candied orange peel (see page 12)

These sliders are a hit with kids. There's just something about the juicy pork, crunchy peanut, and aromatic orange combination they can't resist. The use of candied orange peel as a topping perfectly ties the dish's Asian salty and sweet flavors together.

PREPARATION TIME: 30 MINUTES | MAKES ABOUT 12 SLIDERS

orange and ginger pork sliders with peanut slaw

ORANGE AND GINGER PORK SLIDERS In a large bowl, combine all the ingredients and mix with your hands just to combine. Divide the mixture into 12 small patties. Refrigerate until ready to cook.

PEANUT SLAW In a large bowl, whisk together the peanut butter, shoyu, orange zest, maple syrup, rice vinegar, and garlic. Add the coleslaw mix and toss to coat. Mix in the green onions and peanuts.

Heat the grill to medium-high heat and oil the grate, or set an oiled grill pan over medium-high heat. Grill the patties for 4 minutes on each side, or until cooked through. Toast the slider buns if desired.

Serve the pork sliders generously garnished with peanut slaw and a pinch of candied orange peel.

ORANGE-SESAME FALAFEL

1 (15.5-ounce) can chickpeas, rinsed, drained, and patted dry

1 cup almond flour

$^1/_4$ cup freshly squeezed orange juice (about $^1/_2$ orange)

$^1/_4$ cup chopped fresh cilantro

$^1/_4$ cup chopped fresh flat-leaf parsley

2 tablespoons extra virgin olive oil

1 tablespoon finely grated orange zest (about $^1/_2$ orange)

2 cloves garlic, chopped

1 green onion, chopped

1 teaspoon ground coriander

1 teaspoon baking powder

1 teaspoon kosher salt

Freshly ground black pepper, to taste

$^1/_4$ cup toasted sesame seeds

SPICY TAHINI SAUCE

$^1/_2$ cup Creamy Orange Tahini Dressing (page 16)

$^1/_4$ cup tahini

1 teaspoon sambal oelek

1 teaspoon toasted sesame oil

TO SERVE

Pita bread

I always keep falafel in the freezer: they defrost within minutes in the oven to become a hearty and healthy meal. Serve them as an appetizer, over a salad, or in a pita sandwich. Don't skimp on the spicy tahini sauce: it's dangerously addictive.

PREPARATION TIME: 35 MINUTES PLUS 10 MINUTES FOR COOLING | MAKES ABOUT 24 FALAFEL

orange-sesame falafel with spicy tahini sauce

ORANGE-SESAME FALAFEL Preheat oven to 375°F. Line a baking sheet with parchment paper.

In a food processor, add all the falafel ingredients except the sesame seeds. Pulse, frequently scraping down the sides of the bowl, until you reach a coarse but uniform texture. Remove the bowl from the processor, pull out the blade, and, using a spatula, incorporate the toasted sesame seeds. Using a $^3/_4$-ounce ice cream scoop or your hands, roll the falafel into balls and set onto the baking sheet. Bake for 15–18 minutes, until the falafel are lightly golden and firm to the touch. Let cool for 10 minutes before serving (this will allow the falafel to firm up and reach their ideal texture.)

SPICY TAHINI SAUCE Whisk the dressing with the tahini, sambal oelek, and sesame oil (you can use a blender, stick blender, or food processor to get a perfectly smooth texture). Taste and adjust seasoning, if needed.

Serve the falafel warm with the spicy tahini sauce and toasted pita bread on the side.

The moist texture and spiced flavor of this cake are just irresistible! Wrap the cake and butterscotch sauce jar prettily, and you've got a fabulous edible gift.

PREPARATION TIME: 1 HOUR 25 MINUTES | MAKES 1 LOAF CAKE

orange, date, and walnut cake with orange butterscotch sauce

ORANGE, DATE, AND WALNUT CAKE Preheat oven to 350°F. Generously grease an 9 x 5-inch loaf pan. Line with parchment paper.

Heat the orange juice until hot. Put the dates in a bowl and pour the juice over them. Let dates soak for 10 minutes, stirring from time to time.

In a bowl, whisk the flour, baking powder, baking soda, salt, and cloves together. Set aside. Strain the dates from the orange juice, and set both the juice and the dates aside.

(continued)

ORANGE, DATE, AND
WALNUT CAKE

1 cup freshly squeezed orange juice (about 3 oranges)

2 cups loosely packed chopped pitted dates (about 5.25 ounces)

2 cups all-purpose flour

2 teaspoons baking powder

$1/2$ teaspoon baking soda

$1/2$ teaspoon kosher salt

$1/4$ teaspoon ground cloves

$1/2$ cup (4 ounces) butter, room temperature

$1/2$ cup firmly packed brown sugar

2 eggs

2 teaspoons pure vanilla extract

$1/2$ cup chopped walnuts

2 tablespoons candied orange peel (see page 12) or finely grated orange zest

ORANGE BUTTERSCOTCH SAUCE

1/2 cup (4 ounces) unsalted butter

1 cup firmly packed brown sugar

1/2 cup heavy cream

1/2 cup freshly squeezed orange juice (about 2 oranges)

1 tablespoon Cointreau or Grand Marnier (optional)

1 teaspoon pure vanilla extract

1/4 teaspoon kosher salt

TO SERVE

Candied orange peel (see page 12)

In a large mixing bowl, beat the butter and brown sugar until light and fluffy. Add the eggs, one at a time, beating well between each addition, and then beat in the vanilla. Add one-third of the flour mixture and stir just to combine. Stir in half of the juice. Repeat the steps, ending with the flour mixture. Fold in the dates, walnuts, and candied orange peel. Do not overmix.

Pour the batter into the loaf pan and bake for 60–70 minutes, or until a toothpick inserted into the center comes out clean. (If the top of the cake gets too dark before the end of baking time, loosely cover with aluminum foil and bake until done.) Let cool in the pan for 15 minutes; unmold, set onto a wire rack, and cool completely.

ORANGE BUTTERSCOTCH SAUCE Melt the butter in a heavy-bottom saucepan over medium heat. Add the brown sugar, cream, juice, Cointreau, vanilla, and salt; whisk to combine. Bring to a gentle boil and cook for 10 minutes, stirring occasionally, until the sauce is thick and glossy. Transfer to an airtight jar.

Serve the cake warm or room temperature, generously drizzled with warm sauce. (The sauce may separate after refrigeration. Simply reheat and stir thoroughly before serving.) Top with candied orange peel.

I often find smoothies to be too sweet or thick for my taste. This one falls right in between a fresh juice and a traditional smoothie. It has a bright flavor, a drinkable consistency, and lots of good-for-you ingredients in it. It's a tasty and healthy way to wake up your taste buds!

PREPARATION TIME: 5 MINUTES | MAKES ABOUT 20 OUNCES

bright-and-early orange smoothie

Combine all ingredients in a blender and blend until smooth. Serve immediately.

1 blood or regular orange, peeled and chopped (seeds removed)

$^1/_2$ banana, chopped

$^1/_2$ cup chopped pineapple or mango

$^1/_2$ cup coconut water or coconut milk

Juice from $^1/_2$ lemon

1 tablespoon honey

1 tablespoon hemp seeds (optional)

1 teaspoon finely grated fresh ginger

$^1/_2$ teaspoon ground turmeric

1 cup ice cubes

2 cups freshly squeezed and
    strained blood orange juice
    (about 6 blood oranges)

1 cup Champagne or other
    sparkling white wine

$^1/_4$ cup granulated sugar

$^1/_4$ cup honey

TO SERVE

Pomegranate seeds

Fresh basil leaves

There is no better way to highlight the exceptional flavor and breathtaking color of a blood orange than this chic granita. Serve it for dessert or as a palate cleanser in between the courses of a more elaborate meal.

PREPARATION TIME: 15 MINUTES PLUS AT LEAST 8 HOURS 30 MINUTES FOR COOLING AND FREEZING | SERVES 8

blood orange and champagne granita

Pour the juice and wine into a medium saucepan. Set over medium heat then whisk in the sugar and honey. Bring to a simmer, whisking until the sugar is dissolved. Pour the granita mixture into a square baking pan. Let cool to room temperature, about 30 minutes. Cover with plastic wrap and freeze overnight.

To serve, use a fork to scrape the granita into fluffy ice crystals. Scoop into serving cups, garnish with pomegranate seeds and fresh basil, and serve immediately.

Frangipane is a custard that incorporates ground almonds to produce a toothsome, nutty filling. This tart is spectacular with blood oranges, but if they're off season, substitute clementines.

PREPARATION TIME: 1 HOUR 10 MINUTES | MAKES 1 (9-INCH) TART

blood orange frangipane tart

CRUST Preheat oven to 350°F. Lightly grease a 9-inch tart pan with removable bottom and set on a baking sheet.

In a large bowl, whisk together the flours, sugar, zest, and salt. Drizzle in the butter; stir until the mixture is moist and sticks together. Press the mixture onto the bottom and up the sides of the tart pan. Bake for 20 minutes, or until the crust is lightly golden. Remove from the oven and set aside, leaving the oven on.

FILLING Beat the butter and sugar together until light and fluffy, about 2 minutes. Add the eggs, one at a time, beating well after each addition. Add the flours and almond extract, scraping the sides of the mixing bowl from time to time. Dollop the frangi-pane mixture into the tart shell and smooth the top. Arrange the orange slices over the filling to cover the whole surface.

Bake for about 30 minutes, or until the center of the tart is firm and fully cooked. Remove from the oven and cool completely. If you wish, decorate with sliced almonds before serving. To avoid pushing down the orange slices while cutting, use a very sharp knife to slice. The tart can be made up to a half-day ahead and is best served the day it's made.

CRUST

2 cups almond flour

1 cup all-purpose flour

$1/4$ cup granulated sugar

2 tablespoons finely grated blood orange zest (about 1 blood orange)

$1/4$ teaspoon kosher salt

6 tablespoons (3 ounces) unsalted butter, melted

FILLING

$1/2$ cup (4 ounces) butter, room temperature

$1/2$ cup granulated sugar

2 eggs

1 cup almond flour

$1/4$ cup all-purpose flour

$1/4$ teaspoon almond extract (optional)

3 to 4 blood oranges, peeled and sliced (see page 9)

TO SERVE

Toasted sliced almonds (optional)

mandarin

THE MANDARIN FAMILY of citrus fruits includes several varieties, including tangerines and clementines. The good news is that you can use the varieties interchangeably. Common qualities among these fruits are their petite size, easy-to-peel skin, and incredibly fragrant zest. Mandarins and their cousins routinely play a starring role in desserts, but they're also memorable in marmalades and savory recipes, especially when combined with Asian flavors.

- 4 mandarins, peeled and chopped (seeds removed)
- 4 carrots, peeled and sliced into rounds (about 2 $^1/_2$ cups)
- 2 orange bell peppers, cored and sliced (about 2 cups)
- 2 tablespoons extra virgin olive oil
- 1 teaspoon kosher salt, divided
- $^1/_4$ teaspoon freshly ground black pepper
- 1 shallot, chopped
- $^3/_4$ cup freshly squeezed mandarin juice (about 3 mandarins)
- $^1/_4$ cup extra virgin olive oil
- 2 tablespoons white balsamic vinegar or white wine vinegar
- 1 teaspoon ground turmeric
- $^1/_2$ teaspoon ground ginger
- Pinch of cayenne pepper (optional)

TO SERVE

- Toasted slivered or sliced almonds
- Fresh basil leaves

A classic gazpacho blends raw produce together, but let me assure you—the extra roasting step in this recipe is worth it. The flavors are deepened and concentrated, making the dish fit for year-round dinner parties. No mandarins? You can substitute any orange variety.

PREPARATION TIME: 30 MINUTES PLUS AT LEAST 30 MINUTES FOR REFRIGERATION | SERVES 4

roasted mandarin, carrot, and bell pepper gazpacho

Preheat oven to 450°F. Line a baking sheet with parchment paper. Add the mandarins, carrots, and bell peppers. Drizzle with 2 tablespoons olive oil and season with $^1/_2$ teaspoon salt and the pepper. Toss to coat. Roast for 25 minutes, or until the mandarins and vegetables are soft and charred in spots. Let cool completely.

Transfer the mandarins and vegetables to a blender with the shallot, mandarin juice, $^1/_4$ cup olive oil, remaining salt, vinegar, turmeric, ginger, and cayenne. Blend until very smooth. Adjust the consistency of the gazpacho to your taste by adding more mandarin juice or some water. Transfer to an airtight container and refrigerate for at least 1 hour or overnight.

Serve cool, garnished with almonds and basil.

Buddha bowls are a lasting trend, and with good reason: they're filling, nutritious, and colorful. This bowl is vegan, but you can substitute leftover meat or fish for the tofu.

PREPARATION TIME: 35 MINUTES | SERVES 4

coconut quinoa, crispy tofu, and sweet mandarin buddha bowls

COCONUT QUINOA In a large skillet over medium heat, melt the oil. Add the quinoa and cook, stirring occasionally, until golden, about 3 minutes. Stir in the coconut milk, water, and salt. Bring to a boil, reduce heat to low, cover, and simmer until the liquid is absorbed, about 20 minutes. Remove from heat and let rest for 10 minutes. Fluff with a fork then stir in the coconut.

CRISPY TOFU In a clean skillet over medium heat, melt the oil. In a bowl, toss the tofu in the cornstarch; immediately transfer to the skillet. Sauté, turning the cubes until they're golden brown and crispy all over, about 10 minutes. Season with salt and pepper.

Spoon about 1 cup coconut quinoa into each of 4 large serving bowls. Top with spinach, carrots, and mandarins. Add the crispy tofu, and generously drizzle with dressing. Garnish with fresh cilantro, green onions, and coconut flakes. Serve immediately.

COCONUT QUINOA

1 tablespoon coconut oil or olive oil

1 cup quinoa

1 (13.5-ounce) can coconut milk

$1/2$ cup water

1 teaspoon kosher salt

$1/2$ cup toasted unsweetened shredded coconut

CRISPY TOFU

2 tablespoons coconut oil

1 (12.3-ounce) package extra-firm tofu, drained, pressed dry with paper towels, and cubed

1 tablespoon cornstarch

Sea salt flakes and freshly ground black pepper, to taste

TO ASSEMBLE

2 handfuls baby spinach, coarsely chopped

2 carrots, peeled and shredded (about 1 cup)

4 mandarins, peeled and sliced (see page 9)

Creamy Orange Tahini Dressing (page 16)

Fresh cilantro leaves

2 green onions, sliced

Toasted coconut flakes

GINGER AND MANDARIN PORK

1/4 cup shoyu (Japanese soy sauce)

1 tablespoon honey

1 tablespoon grated fresh ginger

1/4 cup freshly squeezed mandarin juice (about 1 mandarin)

1 tablespoon finely grated mandarin zest (about 1 mandarin)

1/2 teaspoon kosher salt

Freshly ground black pepper, to taste

1 pound pork tenderloin

1 tablespoon olive oil

HERB NOODLE SALAD

About 10 ounces dry Asian-style noodles*

1/2 cup chopped fresh cilantro

1/4 cup chopped fresh basil

1/4 cup chopped fresh mint

2 green onions, sliced

Sea salt flakes, to taste

Freshly ground black pepper, to taste

Though marinating meat requires a bit of planning, you will congratulate yourself for thinking ahead when you enjoy this salty-sweet pork dish. It's delicious hot, but you can also turn it into a cold salad: toss the meat with the dressed noodles and bring it to your next potluck party.

PREPARATION TIME: 50 MINUTES PLUS AT LEAST 1 HOUR FOR MARINATING | SERVES 4

sticky ginger and mandarin pork loin with herb noodle salad

GINGER AND MANDARIN PORK In a small bowl, whisk the shoyu, honey, ginger, juice, zest, salt, and pepper together. Pour into a ziplock bag and add the pork. Toss to coat, seal the bag, and refrigerate. Marinate for at least 1 hour or up to overnight.

Preheat oven to 350°F. In a large ovenproof skillet, heat the olive oil over medium-high heat. Remove the pork from the marinade and shake to let excess drip off; reserve the marinade. Transfer pork to the hot skillet and sear on all sides until golden. Transfer the skillet to the oven. Roast for 20 minutes, or until the internal temperature reaches 145°F.

(continued)

While the pork roasts, pour the marinade into a small saucepan. Bring to a boil, lower the heat, and simmer for 5 minutes, or until thickened. Keep warm.

HERB NOODLE SALAD Bring a large pot of water to a boil. Cook the noodles according to package instructions. Drain then transfer to a large bowl. Drizzle with half of the marinade. Add the cilantro, basil, mint, and onions; toss to combine. Season with salt and pepper.

When the pork is done, brush with the remaining marinade, then transfer to a cutting board, cover with aluminum foil, and let rest for 10 minutes. Thinly slice.

To serve, divide the Herb Noodle Salad between 4 serving bowls. Top with pork loin and drizzle with some marinade.

The quantity of noodles depends on the variety you want to use. Any type of Asian-style noodles (e.g., ramen, udon, soba, stir-fry) will do. Adjust the quantity to serve 4 people, and always cook according to package instructions.

This aromatic pilaf can play sidekick to a variety of dishes: roast chicken, grilled meats and fish, and Indian curries all work, or toss in a can of rinsed and dried chickpeas to turn it into a meal. As with many spiced dishes, it tastes even better the next day.

PREPARATION TIME: 40 MINUTES | SERVES 6

mandarin, almond, and turmeric pilaf

In a large saucepan over medium heat, heat the olive oil until shimmering. Add the onion and sauté until soft. Reduce heat to medium low. Add the garlic, turmeric, salt, ginger, and cloves; stir for 1 minute, or until fragrant.

Add the rice and cook for 2 minutes, stirring constantly. Add the broth and the raisins. Bring to a boil, reduce heat, cover, and simmer for 20 minutes, or until the broth is fully absorbed. Remove from heat and let rest, covered, for 10 minutes.

Fluff the rice with a fork and transfer to a large serving bowl. Add the mandarin pieces, almonds, and green onions. Toss to combine and serve.

1 tablespoon olive oil

1 small onion, minced

2 cloves garlic, minced

2 teaspoons turmeric

$1/2$ teaspoon kosher salt

$1/2$ teaspoon ground ginger

$1/4$ teaspoon ground cloves

1 cup basmati rice, rinsed thoroughly

2 cups vegetable or chicken broth

$1/2$ cup golden raisins

3 mandarins, peeled and chopped (seeds removed)

$1/2$ cup slivered almonds

2 green onions, sliced

- 3.5 ounces dark chocolate, chopped
- $1/4$ cup granulated sugar
- 1 teaspoon cornstarch
- 4 egg yolks
- 1 cup milk
- 1 cup heavy cream
- 1 tablespoon Cointreau or Grand Marnier (optional)
- 1 tablespoon finely grated mandarin zest (about 1 mandarin)
- $1/4$ cup fruity, best-quality extra virgin olive oil

TO SERVE

- Whipped cream
- Mandarin segments (see page 9)
- Chopped pistachios

Pots de crème (literally, cream jars) are one of my favorite desserts to serve to company. This delightfully silky version gets a flavor boost from olive oil and fresh mandarins.

PREPARATION TIME: 15 MINUTES PLUS 2 HOURS FOR REFRIGERATION | SERVES 6

dark chocolate and mandarin pots de crème

Place the chocolate in a large bowl and set a strainer over the top.

Combine the sugar and cornstarch in a saucepan. Whisk in the egg yolks; then add the milk, cream, Cointreau, and zest. Place over medium heat and bring to a boil, whisking constantly and scraping down the sides and bottom of the pan so the mixture doesn't stick. Once the mixture boils, reduce heat to low and simmer for 1–2 minutes, whisking constantly, until thickened.

Strain liquid into the bowl containing the chopped chocolate. Let sit for 1 minute then whisk until smooth. Add the oil and whisk until well incorporated. Divide between 6 (1-cup) serving glasses or bowls. Cover with plastic wrap and refrigerate for 2 hours, or until the chocolate cream is completely cool.

Bring the pots de crème back to room temperature 15–30 minutes before serving. Garnish each portion with whipped cream, mandarin segments, and chopped pistachios.

Sneaking squash into dessert might sound surprising, but just think of carrot cake! In this recipe, both squash and clementine make the cupcakes wonderfully moist, and their flavors marry with maple syrup perfectly. If you can't find maple sugar for the buttercream, substitute powdered sugar.

PREPARATION TIME: 40 MINUTES | MAKES 36 MINI CUPCAKES

squash and clementine mini cupcakes with maple buttercream

1 1/4 cups all-purpose flour

1 teaspoon baking powder

1/2 teaspoon ground ginger

1/4 teaspoon salt

2 eggs

3/4 cup firmly packed brown sugar

1/3 cup canola oil

1/4 cup freshly squeezed, strained clementine juice (about 2 clementines)

1 tablespoon finely grated clementine zest (about 2 clementines)

1 teaspoon pure vanilla extract

1/2 cup grated butternut squash or pumpkin (about 2.5 ounces)

CUPCAKES Preheat oven to 350°F. Line a mini muffin pan with paper liners.

In large bowl, whisk the flour, baking powder, ginger, and salt together. In another bowl, beat the eggs, brown sugar, and oil together for 2 minutes. Add the juice, zest, and vanilla and whisk to incorporate. Pour the liquid ingredients into the dry ingredients and mix just until combined. Fold in the squash.

Divide the batter between the muffin cups, filling each three-fourths full. Bake for 16 minutes, or until a toothpick inserted into the center comes out clean. Let cool for 10 minutes, and then transfer to a wire rack to cool completely.

(continued)

MAPLE BUTTERCREAM

$^1/_2$ cup (4 ounces) butter, room
   temperature

2 tablespoons pure maple syrup

2 cups powdered sugar

$^1/_2$ cup granulated maple sugar

$^1/_4$ cup heavy cream

TO SERVE

Coarse maple sugar

Clementine zest

MAPLE BUTTERCREAM Beat the butter until creamy. Drizzle in the maple syrup and beat until fully incorporated. Add the powdered sugar and maple sugar and mix on low speed to combine. Increase the speed and beat until smooth. Add the cream and beat at high speed until the frosting is light and fluffy.

Use a pastry spatula or a pastry bag fitted with a round or star tip to pipe the frosting onto the cupcakes. Garnish each cupcake with coarse maple sugar and clementine zest. The frosted cupcakes can be refrigerated in an airtight container for up to 3 days, or frozen for up to 1 month. Always return the cupcakes to room temperature before serving.

Note: For standard-size cupcakes, simply line regular muffin cups with paper liners, fill each three-fourths full, and bake for 24 minutes, or until a toothpick inserted in the center of a cupcake comes out clean.

Who has time to fuss over breakfast on a weekday? I sure don't, and this recipe is my tastiest time-saver. Throw these overnight oats together on Sunday night and enjoy brightly flavored, filling breakfasts all week long.

PREPARATION TIME: 45 MINUTES PLUS AT LEAST 8 HOURS FOR REFRIGERATION | SERVES 6

protein-packed clementine overnight oats

1 cup regular oats

1 1/2 cups freshly squeezed clementine juice (about 12 clementines) or orange juice (about 3 oranges)

1 cup vanilla Greek yogurt

1/2 cup coarsely chopped pistachios or walnuts

1/2 cup chopped dried cranberries

1/4 cup hemp or chia seeds

1 1/2 tablespoons finely grated clementine zest (about 2 clementines)

3 clementines, peeled and chopped (seeds removed)

TO SERVE

Toasted pumpkin seeds

Honey

Place the oats and juice in a bowl, cover with plastic wrap, and allow to stand for 15 minutes, or until the oats have fully absorbed the juice. Mix in the yogurt, pistachios, cranberries, hemp seeds, and zest. Fold in the clementine pieces. Transfer to an airtight container and refrigerate overnight.

To serve, spoon into a serving bowl and top with toasted pumpkin seeds and a drizzle of honey. The prepared oats will keep refrigerated for up to 5 days.

CRUST

1 cup graham cracker crumbs

$^1/_2$ cup ground toasted hazelnuts (about 1.4 ounces)

$^1/_4$ cup granulated sugar

$^1/_4$ cup (2 ounces) butter, melted

FILLING

20 ounces ricotta cheese (about 2 $^1/_4$ cups)

$^3/_4$ cup granulated sugar

3 eggs

2 tablespoons all-purpose flour

2 teaspoons finely grated mandarin zest (about 1 mandarin)

$^1/_4$ cup freshly squeezed, strained mandarin juice (about 1 mandarin)

1 teaspoon pure vanilla extract

TO SERVE

12 ounces fresh raspberries (about 2 $^1/_4$ cups)

Chopped toasted hazelnuts

Mandarin zest

Berries and mandarins have a way of complementing each other, both in flavor and color. In this recipe, hazelnut joins the duo to create a delightfully fresh dessert.

PREPARATION TIME: 1 HOUR 10 MINUTES | SERVES 8 TO 12

mandarin and raspberry ricotta tart

CRUST Preheat oven to 350°F. Grease a 10-inch tart pan with removable bottom, or a 9-inch springform pan and set on a baking sheet.

In a large mixing bowl, whisk together the graham cracker crumbs, hazelnuts, and sugar. Drizzle in the butter and stir until the mixture is moist and sticks together when pressed. Press the crust into the bottom of the prepared pan. Bake for 20 minutes, or until crust is fragrant and edges are lightly golden. Let cool completely.

FILLING In a food processor, combine all the filling ingredients together; process until the texture is smooth and silky. Pour the filling onto the tart shell and smooth out the top. Bake for 35-40 minutes, or until the tart is set and golden around the edges but still a bit wet and jiggly in the center (the filling will fully set as the tart cools). Let cool completely to room temperature, and then refrigerate for at least 1 hour or overnight.

To serve, unmold the tart and transfer to a serving plate. Sprinkle the top of the tart with the raspberries. Garnish with hazelnuts and mandarin zest, and serve.

grapefruit and pomelo

GRAPEFRUITS ARE A COMMON SIGHT on the breakfast table, but a lot of us forget to cook and bake with them–that needs to change! Their bright color and delightfully puckery taste make them perfect for salads and baked goods. Make sure to pick up a pomelo when the season comes: one fruit goes a long way–it's the largest of all citrus fruits–and its honeyed flavor makes it great for salsas, marmalades, and candies, or as a fresh topping for creamy desserts.

2 very ripe avocados, peeled and
   pitted

$1/4$ cup freshly squeezed lemon
   juice (about 1 lemon)

2 tablespoons extra virgin
   olive oil

1 tablespoon chopped fresh
   cilantro

$1/2$ teaspoon kosher salt

Freshly ground black pepper,
   to taste

7 ounces crabmeat, fresh or
   defrosted, patted dry

1 pomelo, peeled, segmented
   (see page 9), and diced

TO SERVE

Extra virgin olive oil

Sea salt flakes

Freshly ground black pepper

Fresh cilantro leaves

Verrines are quite popular in France. The name describes
food, sweet or savory, prettily layered in glass containers. This
presentation technique showcases the salad's soft tones of
green, pink, and yellow especially well.

PREPARATION TIME: 20 MINUTES | SERVES 4

crab, pomelo, and whipped avocado verrines

In a food processor, combine the avocados, lemon juice, olive oil,
cilantro, salt, and pepper. Process until creamy, scraping down
the bowl from time to time to thoroughly incorporate all of the
ingredients. Divide between 4 serving glasses. Top with crabmeat
and pomelo. Finish with a drizzle of olive oil, a sprinkle of sea salt,
pepper, and cilantro leaves. Serve, or refrigerate for up to a half-day.

Inspired by a classic Sicilian recipe, this colorful salad is the perfect combination of bright, mellow, sour, and salty. Enjoy this salad in the heart of winter to wake up your senses, or serve on a hot summer night with a glass of rosé.

PREPARATION TIME: 15 MINUTES | SERVES 4

grapefruit, fennel, and parmesan salad

1 fennel bulb, thinly sliced

2 pink grapefruits, peeled and segmented (see page 9)

2 handfuls soft-tasting, light-weight greens (baby spinach, mâche, or pea shoots)

Everyday Citrus Dressing (grape-fruit variation, page 16)

Sea salt flakes, to taste

Freshly ground black pepper, to taste

Shaved Parmigiano-Reggiano cheese

Combine the fennel, grapefruits, and greens in a large salad bowl. Drizzle with 3 tablespoons dressing. Season with salt and pepper. Taste, and add more dressing or adjust seasoning if needed. Garnish with Parmigiano-Reggiano and serve immediately.

AVOCADO-GRAPEFRUIT SALSA

2 tablespoons olive oil

1 teaspoon honey

1/2 teaspoon ground cumin

1/2 teaspoon sea salt flakes

1 ripe avocado, peeled, pitted, and diced

1 large pink grapefruit, peeled, segmented (see page 9), and diced

2 tablespoons finely chopped red onion

1 tablespoon finely chopped jalapeño pepper (about 1/2 pepper)

BROILED FISH

2 teaspoons Mexican chili powder (see page 49)

1 teaspoon dried oregano

1 teaspoon kosher salt

1/2 teaspoon freshly ground black pepper

1 pound skinned firm fish (tilapia, halibut, mahi mahi, or salmon), cut into strips

TO SERVE

8 whole-wheat tortillas

Plain Greek yogurt or sour cream

Microgreens

Minced green onions

Fresh cilantro leaves

I like tacos, but I *love* fish tacos because they come together so quickly. In this recipe, the fish is coated in aromatic spices and broiled in just a few minutes–just the time it takes to assemble the zesty salsa.

PREPARATION TIME: 25 MINUTES | MAKES 8 TACOS

broiled fish tacos with avocado-grapefruit salsa

AVOCADO-GRAPEFRUIT SALSA In a large bowl, whisk together the olive oil, honey, cumin, and salt. Add the avocado, grapefruit, onion, and jalapeño. Toss to coat and set aside while you prepare the fish.

BROILED FISH Set a rack in the upper third of the oven and pre-heat the broiler on high. Cover a baking sheet with aluminum foil and lightly coat with oil.

In a bowl, combine the chili powder, oregano, salt, and pepper. Add the fish and rub the spices all over. Transfer to the prepared baking sheet. Lightly spray the fish with cooking spray. Broil just until the fish is cooked through and charred in spots, 5-7 minutes, depending on the fish you're using.

To serve, smear the tortillas with some Greek yogurt or sour cream. Add some broiled fish and a few spoonfuls of salsa. Garnish with microgreens, green onions, and cilantro.

Upside-down cake has a bit of a vintage charm, so I like to switch things up by incorporating unexpected fruits. In this spectacular case, pink grapefruit glimmers through the velvety caramel, which also seeps into the cake to keep a perfect balance of bitter and sweet.

PREPARATION TIME: 45 MINUTES | MAKES 1 (9-INCH) CAKE

grapefruit upside-down cake

CARAMEL In a saucepan over medium heat, whisk the butter, brown sugar, honey, Campari, and vanilla until the mixture is smooth. Bring to a full boil and cook for 3 minutes, until thick. Remove from heat, cover, and set aside.

CAKE Preheat oven to 350°F. Lightly oil a 9-inch springform pan. Wrap the outside of the pan with a sheet of aluminum foil (to avoid leaks) and set over a baking sheet.

In a small bowl, whisk the flour, baking powder, and salt together and set aside. In a large mixing bowl, beat the butter and sugar until light and fluffy, about 2 minutes. Add the eggs, one at a time, beating well between each addition. Scrape down the sides of the bowl, and then beat in the vanilla. Add one-third of the dry ingredients and stir just to combine. Stir in half of the milk. Repeat the steps, ending with the dry ingredients. Do not overmix.

(continued)

CARAMEL

$1/2$ cup (4 ounces) unsalted butter

1 cup firmly packed brown sugar

2 tablespoons honey

1 tablespoon Campari or Aperol (optional)

$1/2$ vanilla bean, halved and seeds scraped, or 2 teaspoons pure vanilla extract

$1/2$ cup freshly squeezed grapefruit juice*

CAKE

$1 1/2$ cups all-purpose flour

2 teaspoons baking powder

$1/4$ teaspoon kosher salt

$1/4$ cup (2 ounces) butter, room temperature

$1/2$ cup granulated sugar

2 eggs

1 teaspoon pure vanilla extract

$3/4$ cup milk

4 to 5 grapefruits, peeled and segmented (see page 9)*

2 teaspoons cornstarch

1 teaspoon freshly squeezed,
strained lemon juice

$^1/_2$ vanilla bean, seeds scraped,
or 1 teaspoon pure vanilla
extract

3 egg whites, room temperature

$^3/_4$ cup granulated sugar

TOPPING

2 pink grapefruits, peeled and
segmented (see page 9)

1 tablespoon honey

1 cup whipping cream

2 tablespoons granulated sugar

$^1/_2$ cup fresh pomegranate seeds

$^1/_4$ cup shelled pistachios

Bring a Pavlova to the dinner table, and you're sure to make an impression. You'll need to prepare the meringue base several hours ahead or, ideally, the night before, so it has time to dry thoroughly and acquire that signature crunch.

PREPARATION TIME: 1 HOUR 40 MINUTES PLUS AT LEAST 3 HOURS COOLING TIME | SERVES 6

grapefruit and pomegranate pavlova

MERINGUE Preheat oven to 250°F. Line a baking sheet with parchment paper. Using a pencil, trace an 8-inch circle over the parchment paper; flip it over to use as a template (you should see the circle through the paper).

In a small bowl, combine the cornstarch, lemon juice, and vanilla. Set aside. Whisk the egg whites until stiff peaks form, and then whisk in the sugar, 1 tablespoon at a time, until fully incorporated. Then whisk until the meringue is glossy and returns to stiff peaks. Whisk in the cornstarch mixture, and then whip for a few seconds until fully incorporated.

Transfer the meringue mixture onto the prepared baking sheet and spread into a circle, making the sides a bit higher than the center to create a well. Bake for 1 hour 30 minutes. Then turn the oven off and let the meringue cool completely in the oven, 3 hours to overnight.

TOPPING Place the grapefruit segments in a bowl and drizzle with the honey. Stir to coat. Let rest for 15 minutes at room temperature.

Set the meringue on a serving plate. In a bowl, whip the cream with the sugar until soft peaks form. Fill the meringue well with the whipped cream. Generously garnish with grapefruit segments, pomegranate seeds, and pistachios. Serve immediately.

PANNA COTTA

1 1/2 cups milk, divided

1 tablespoon unflavored
    powdered gelatin
    (1 2.8-ounce packet)

1 1/2 cups heavy cream

1/3 cup pure maple syrup

1 teaspoon pure vanilla extract

COCONUT CRUMBLE

1/4 cup all-purpose flour

1/4 cup coconut sugar or
    granulated sugar

1/4 cup toasted unsweetened
    shredded coconut

2 tablespoons coconut oil,
    melted

TOPPING

1 pomelo, peeled, segmented
    (see page 9) and diced

1 tablespoon pure maple syrup

Panna cotta is deceptively quick and easy to prepare, and topping it with fresh fruit and a crunchy element pushes the dessert to fine dining levels. Mild-tasting pomelo is a perfect match for the creamy base and aromatic coconut topping, but if you can't find it, substitute diced Cara Cara or blood oranges.

PREPARATION TIME: 50 MINUTES PLUS AT LEAST 4 HOURS FOR REFRIGERATION | SERVES 6

pomelo-maple panna cotta with coconut crumble

PANNA COTTA Pour 1/2 cup of the milk into a large bowl. Sprinkle the gelatin over the milk and let rest for 5 minutes (don't mix).

Pour the remaining milk and the cream in a saucepan. Whisk in the maple syrup and vanilla. Warm the mixture over medium heat until piping hot (no need to simmer or boil).

Pour the very hot milk mixture over the gelatin and whisk until completely dissolved. Divide the panna cotta mixture between 6 glasses, small bowls, or ramekins. Cover with plastic wrap and refrigerate for at least 4 hours to set.

COCONUT CRUMBLE Preheat oven to 350°F. Line a baking sheet with parchment paper. In a large bowl, mix the flour, coconut sugar, and toasted coconut together. Using a fork, mix the oil into the coconut mixture until evenly crumbly. Spread the mixture on the baking sheet and bake for 10 minutes, until the crumbs are golden (toss the crumbs 2 or 3 times during baking to brown evenly). Let cool completely. Store the crumble in an airtight container at room temperature until ready to use. (The crumble will keep for up to 3 days.)

TOPPING In a small bowl, combine the diced pomelo and maple syrup. Spoon some of the pomelo over each panna cotta. Just before serving, generously sprinkle each panna cotta with coconut crumble.

GRAPEFRUIT CUPCAKES

1 1/2 cups all-purpose flour

1 teaspoon baking powder

1/4 teaspoon kosher salt

2 eggs

1 cup sugar

1/2 cup canola oil

1/4 cup milk

1/4 cup freshly squeezed, strained pink grapefruit juice (about 1/2 grapefruit)

1 tablespoon finely grated pink grapefruit zest (about 1/2 grapefruit)

1 teaspoon pure vanilla extract

MERINGUE FROSTING

3 egg whites

1/4 teaspoon cream of tartar

1/2 teaspoon pure vanilla extract

1/2 cup granulated sugar

FILLING

Pink grapefruit curd (see page 18)

If you love lemon meringue desserts, you'll love this grapefruit variation on the theme. The flavor of grapefruit mellows once cooked, providing a balanced kick to both the cupcakes and the curd. The sweet cloud of meringue rounds things off beautifully. For a quicker treat, you can leave out the curd filling.

PREPARATION TIME: 1 HOUR 10 MINUTES | MAKES 12 MUFFINS

grapefruit cupcakes with toasted meringue frosting

GRAPEFRUIT CUPCAKES Preheat oven to 325°F. Line a 12-cup muffin pan with paper liners.

In a bowl, sift together the flour, baking powder, and salt.

In another bowl, beat the eggs and sugar together until pale and fluffy, about 2 minutes. Whisk in the oil, milk, juice, zest, and vanilla. Add the flour mixture and mix until just combined.

Divide the batter evenly among lined cups, leaving 1/4-inch at the top. Bake, rotating the pan halfway through the cooking time, until cupcakes are golden brown and a toothpick inserted in the center comes out clean, about 25 minutes. Transfer the pan to a wire rack to cool completely before removing the cupcakes.

MERINGUE Whip the egg whites with the cream of tartar and vanilla until soft peaks form. Add the sugar, 1 tablespoon at a time, until the meringue is glossy and stiff peaks form.

TO ASSEMBLE Cut out a small round from the top of each cupcake. Pipe some grapefruit curd inside, and then replace the cut-out piece over the curd. Fill a pastry bag fitted with a large open star tip with the meringue. Pipe the frosting onto each cupcake, so as to cover the grapefruit curd (you can also simply spoon the meringue over each cupcake). Broil for a few seconds in the oven to brown the meringue (keep an eye on the process at all times as browning occurs quickly), or use a small kitchen torch: hold it 3-4 inches from surface of frosting, and wave it back and forth until frosting is lightly browned all over (be careful to keep the flame away from the paper liner).

Serve the cupcakes immediately, or store in an airtight container for up to 1 day.

kumquat, yuzu, and more

THERE ARE SO MANY other varieties of citrus fruits to play with; from festive kumquats to rare yuzu fruit to exotic orange blossom water and preserved lemons–the possibilities are endless. If you see a new-to-you citrus variety at the market, take a chance on it! The recipes in this chapter include substitution options. In all cases, you can still make the dish using alternate ingredients if you can't find the main ingredient. Consider it my push to make you citrus adventurous–you can't go wrong.

ROASTED BEETS

4 large red or yellow beets, scrubbed, peeled, and quartered

1 tablespoon olive oil

2 unpeeled kumquats, halved, seeded, and minced

SALAD

2 handfuls arugula

20 unpeeled kumquats, quartered and seeded

Everyday Citrus Dressing (orange variation, page 16)

$1/2$ teaspoon sea salt flakes, plus more to taste

Freshly ground black pepper, to taste

8 ounces fresh mozzarella cheese (preferably mozzarella di bufala), room temperature

$1/2$ cup coarsely chopped walnuts

$1/4$ cup fresh basil leaves

2 tablespoons minced fresh chives

Serving salad in the winter can be unexpectedly comforting, especially when it includes roasted beets, zesty kumquats, and creamy mozzarella. This salad is nourishing enough to be served as a main course or split it into six portions to enjoy as a colorful appetizer.

PREPARATION TIME: 1 HOUR 15 MINUTES | SERVES 4 TO 6

roasted beet, kumquat, and fresh mozzarella salad

ROASTED BEETS Preheat the oven to 400°F. Line a baking sheet with aluminum foil and lightly coat with oil. Add the beets, olive oil, and minced kumquats; toss to combine. Gather and lift the corners of the aluminum foil, drizzle 2 tablespoons of water over the beets, and then twist the foil shut to create a closed packet that will help steam the beets. Roast for 45–60 minutes, or until the beets can easily be pierced with a knife. Transfer the beets to a large bowl and let cool completely.

SALAD Add the arugula and kumquats to the beets. Drizzle with $1/4$ cup dressing, sprinkle with salt and pepper, and toss to coat. Transfer to a large serving plate. Top with torn pieces of mozzarella, walnuts, basil, and chives. Drizzle with more dressing and season with a pinch of sea salt flakes. Serve immediately.

24 kumquats*

1/4 cup (2 ounces) unsalted butter

1/4 cup tahini

3/4 cup almond flour

1/2 cup all-purpose flour

1/2 cup cane sugar or regular granulated sugar

1/2 cup firmly packed brown sugar

1/4 cup toasted sesame seeds

1/2 teaspoon baking powder

5 egg whites (freshly separated, or from a carton)

This creative take on the classic French mini cake has a textbook texture underscored by the flavor of nutty tahini and sweet-and-sour kumquats. If kumquats are off-season, you can substitute any citrus zest. The result will be different but delicious all the same.

PREPARATION: 36 MINUTES | MAKES 24 FINANCIERS

sesame kumquat financiers

Slice off both ends of each kumquat. Thinly slice 6 kumquats, seeding as you go, and set aside. Seed and mince the remaining kumquats, and set aside separately.

Set a rack in the upper third of the oven, and a second rack in the lower third. Preheat to 350°F. Generously grease 2 (12-cup) muffin pans.** Sprinkle with flour and tap out the excess. Alternatively, you can line the muffin pans with parchment paper cups.

Warm the butter and tahini together just until the butter is melted. Stir until combined.

In a large bowl, whisk together the almond flour, all-purpose flour, granulated sugar, brown sugar, sesame seeds, and baking powder. Add the egg whites and whisk until fully incorporated and the mixture is thick and sticky. Whisk in the butter-tahini mixture. Fold in the minced kumquats.

Drop 1 tablespoonful of dough into each prepared muffin cup. Arrange a few kumquat slices over each financier. Place the first pan on the upper rack and the second one on the lower rack. Bake for 16 minutes, swapping and rotating the pans halfway through, until the financiers are golden brown around the edges. Let cool for 10 minutes in the pan. Run a sharp knife around each financier and carefully pull them out of the pan. Transfer to a wire rack to cool completely.

Financiers are at their very best when freshly baked, but you can refrigerate them in an airtight container for up to 3 days. Return to room temperature before eating.

If you can't find kumquats, substitute $^1/_4$ cup finely grated zest of your choice: orange (about 2), mandarin (about 4), or clementines (about 6). If desired, you can top each financier with a very thin piece of fruit to decorate.

**If you don't have 2 muffin pans, prepare the financiers in two batches. Simply cover and refrigerate the leftover batter in between batches and add a couple minutes to the baking time of the second batch. Alternatively, you can also use a 24-cup mini muffin pan.*

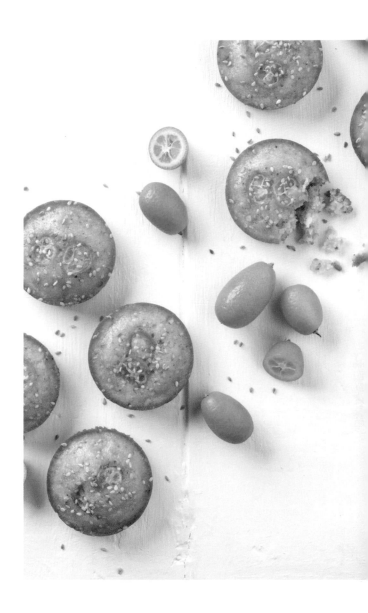

These beautiful black and yellow cookies have a buttery texture that melts in your mouth and delightfully contrasts with the tart curd that adorns them. If you can't find fresh yuzu, use bottled yuzu juice, or simply substitute regular lemon curd.

PREPARATION TIME: 35 MINUTES | MAKES 50 COOKIES

sesame thumbprint cookies with yuzu curd

Using a mortar and pestle or a coffee grinder, grind $1/4$ cup of the sesame seeds and set aside. Preheat oven to 350°F. Line a baking sheet with parchment paper and set aside.

Beat the butter and tahini together until creamy. Add the brown sugar and beat until well incorporated, about 2 minutes. Add the egg and mix to incorporate. Add the flour, ground sesame seeds, zest, and salt; mix until no trace of flour is visible.

Pour the remaining sesame seeds in a shallow bowl. Use a 2-teaspoon cookie scoop to form a ball of dough. Roll dough in seeds then transfer to the prepared baking sheet, flattening slightly. Press your thumb into the center of the ball to create a deep indentation. Repeat to form all cookies, spacing 2 inches apart.

Bake for 15 minutes, or until the cookies are firm and slightly golden around the edges. Let cool on the baking sheet for 5 minutes then transfer to a wire rack to cool completely. Just before serving, garnish with yuzu curd.

$3/4$ cup black sesame seeds, divided

1 cup (8 ounces) butter, room temperature

$1/4$ cup tahini, room temperature

$1/2$ cup firmly packed brown sugar

1 egg

$2 1/2$ cups all-purpose flour

1 teaspoon finely grated yuzu or lemon zest

$1/4$ teaspoon salt

1 batch yuzu or lemon curd (page 18, about 12 ounces)

- 1/4 cup chopped preserved lemon rind, pulp discarded* (see page 15)
- 1/4 cup freshly squeezed lemon juice (about 1 lemon)
- 1 1/2 cups heavy cream
- 5 egg yolks
- 1 cup granulated sugar, divided

I won't mince my words: you should only make this recipe with homemade preserved lemons (see page 15), or ones that come from a trusted store or manufacturer, as your choice can make or break the dish. Preserved lemons have a compelling savory quality, which cuts through the cream and sweetness of the dish to create an unforgettable dessert.

PREPARATION TIME: 1 HOUR PLUS AT LEAST 3 HOURS FOR REFRIGERATION | SERVES 6

preserved lemon crème brûlée

Preheat oven to 300°F. Set a shallow baking or roasting pan close to the oven, and place 6 (3/4-cup) ramekins or small bowls into the pan. Bring a kettle of water to a boil and keep warm.

Purée the preserved lemon rind and lemon juice together. In a saucepan set over medium heat, bring the cream and preserved lemon mixture to a simmer. Remove from heat.

In a mixing bowl, beat the egg yolks and 1/2 cup of the sugar together until well-combined and pale yellow. While constantly whisking, gradually pour the warm cream mixture in a thin stream into the egg mixture. **NOTE:** It's essential to *very slowly* pour the warm liquid into the eggs to avoid curdling them. Pass the mixture through a sieve and into a measuring cup.

Pour 1 inch of hot water from the kettle into the roasting pan, around the ramekins. Carefully pour the custard into the prepared ramekins. Transfer the roasting pan to the oven, making sure to remain steady so the water doesn't splash into the ramekins. Bake for 30 minutes, or until the crèmes are set around the edges but still a bit jiggly in the center (they will set completely while cooling). Transfer the ramekins to a wire rack and let cool to room temperature. Cover with plastic wrap and refrigerate for at least 3 hours, or overnight.

Right before caramelizing, sprinkle a generous tablespoonful of sugar over each crème, shaking and swirling the ramekins to spread the sugar evenly. The sugar must form a thin, even layer over the crèmes.

If using a blowtorch, make sure to caramelize the crèmes right as they come out of the refrigerator. If using a broiler, place the crèmes in the freezer for 20 minutes before caramelizing so they remain at the right temperature and consistency.

BLOWTORCH TECHNIQUE Start with the flame about 6 inches away from the surface, constantly moving your hand in a circle over the ramekins. Gradually move closer to the sugar as you start seeing it liquefy. Make sure not to remain in a single spot for too long so you don't burn the surface. The crackly surface is done when it's shiny and a lovely golden caramel color. Repeat for all servings. Serve immediately.

BROILER TECHNIQUE Place a rack at the top position in your oven and preheat the broiler on high. Set the ramekins on a baking sheet and place on the top rack, keeping the oven half open so you can carefully watch over the caramelization of the crust. Because broilers vary in strength and size, you should rotate the baking sheet at least once during the process and even shuffle the ramekins so the crusts caramelize evenly. Remove from the oven and serve immediately.

Crèmes brûlées should be served cool or at room temperature.

If you don't have preserved lemon on hand, substitute 2 tablespoons finely grated lemon zest (about 2 lemons).

2 cups quartered or halved strawberries

1 tablespoon orange blossom honey or any other honey variety

ORANGE BLOSSOM ZABAGLIONE

4 egg yolks

$1/4$ cup Cointreau, or freshly squeezed, strained orange juice

2 tablespoons honey

1 teaspoon orange blossom water

Pinch of kosher salt

$1/2$ cup heavy cream

TO SERVE

Ground pistachios

An Italian dessert, zabaglione is essentially a dreamily light custard made with egg yolks, sugar, and liqueur or sweet wine. In this version, folding whipped cream into the cooked custard stabilizes it, allowing you to make the dessert a few hours in advance. The sweet floral flavor of orange blossom exquisitely complements fresh strawberries, but you could also use other fresh berries, or even grilled apricots or peaches.

PREPARATION TIME: 35 MINUTES | SERVES 4

orange blossom zabaglione with strawberries

STRAWBERRIES In a small bowl, combine the strawberries and honey; toss to coat. Let rest at room temperature for 15–30 minutes.

ZABAGLIONE Whisk the egg yolks, Cointreau, honey, orange blossom water, and salt in a heatproof bowl. Set the bowl over a pan of simmering water. Beat continuously until double in volume, about 5 minutes. Remove from heat.

Whisk the heavy cream until stiff peaks form. Using a spatula, gently fold the whipped cream into the custard until combined. Refrigerate the zabaglione for 15 minutes, or up to 6 hours.

Divide the strawberries among 4 serving bowls. Spoon the zabaglione in with the strawberries, sprinkle with pistachios, and serve immediately.

index

Metric Conversion Chart

VOLUME MEASUREMENTS		WEIGHT MEASUREMENTS		TEMPERATURE CONVERSION	
U.S.	METRIC	U.S.	METRIC	FAHRENHEIT	CELSIUS
1 teaspoon	5 ml	1/2 ounce	15 g	250	120
1 tablespoon	15 ml	1 ounce	30 g	300	150
1/4 cup	60 ml	3 ounces	90 g	325	160
1/3 cup	75 ml	4 ounces	115 g	350	180
1/2 cup	125 ml	8 ounces	225 g	375	190
2/3 cup	150 ml	12 ounces	350 g	400	200
3/4 cup	175 ml	1 pound	450 g	425	220
1 cup	250 ml	2 1/4 pounds	1 kg	450	230